Great Smoky Mountains National Park

ANGLER'S COMPANION

*A complete fishing guide to
America's most popular national park*

Ian Rutter

Great Smoky Mountains National Park

ANGLER'S COMPANION

*A complete fishing guide to
America's most popular national park*

Ian Rutter

Frank **A**mato
PORTLAND

Biography

Ian Rutter grew up in East Tennessee not far from the Great Smoky Mountains. He took up fly fishing when he attended the University of Tennessee at Knoxville where he studied botany and zoology. Upon graduation he decided that fly fishing was where his future lay. Ian moved to Townsend and became a fishing guide on Little River. He later managed a fly shop in Townsend. Ian is now a freelance outdoor writer and photographer, traveling with his wife Charity across the country in constant search of new fishing destinations. They own and operate R&R Fly Fishing Smoky Mountain Guide Service in Townsend, Tennessee. www.RandRFlyFishing.com

Dedication

First and foremost I must thank my wife Charity for all of her love and encouragement on this project. Her companionship and help have made this a true labor of love. I must also extend my gratitude to Jack Gregory, Tim Doyle, and Walter Babb. These men have given me an appreciation for Smoky Mountain trout and the local heritage of fly fishing. There are countless other fly fishers whose company I've enjoyed and I must thank them for the good times we've shared. Finally, I'd like to thank Steve Moore, Matt Kulp and all the members on the fisheries crew at Great Smoky Mountains National Park. They have been very free with their knowledge and findings in the park.

Photography: Ian and Charity Rutter unless otherwise noted.
Fly Plate Photography: Jim Schollmeyer
Design: Jerry Hutchinson & Charity Rutter

Softbound ISBN-13: 978-1-57188-241-7
Softbound UPC: 0-66066-00495-6

Frank Amato Publications, Inc.
P.O. Box 82112, Portland, Oregon 97282
(503) 653-8108
Printed in Hong Kong
3 5 7 9 10 8 6 4

Table of Contents

Part I: Fishing the Great Smoky Mountains

Part II: Stream Descriptions

Legend

———	Paved Road
═══	Gravel Road
———	National Park Boundary
━━━	Water
———	Stream Closed to Fishing
—·—·—	State Line
· · · · ·	Trail - Horses Prohibited
·········	Trail - Horses Permitted
⛺	Developed National Park Campground

Great Smoky Mountains National Park

N
W · E
S

321
Foothills Parkway
40
Cosby

321
441
321
Gatlinburg
Cosby
TN
NC
Big Creek
40

321
Townsend
321
Greenbriar

Foothills Parkway
Little River Roa
Tremont   Elkmont
Newfound
441
TN
NC
Cataloochee

Abrams Creek
Cades Cove
441
Gap Road
Balsam Mtn
276

Parson Branch Rd
TN
NC
Clingmans Dome
Smokemont
Maggie Valley

129
TN
NC
Blue Ridge
Cherokee
Parkway

Calderwood Lake
28
Deep Creek
19
19

Cheoah Lake
Fontana Dam   Cable Cove USFS   Fontana Lake
Bryson City
441

129
74

Part 1: Fishing the Great Smoky Mountains
Introduction

I have been fishing the streams of Great Smoky Mountains National Park for ten years, and when I say ten years, I don't mean on a few occasions a year. Since I have always lived close to the park I have been fortunate enough to fish it several times a week year round. In fact, I was researching this book long before I knew I would write it.

Valuable lessons have been learned over the years. Most of what I have learned has come from spending time on the stream in all sorts of conditions, drought and flood, the dog days of summer, and cold snowy days. Many miles were walked just to find the next good run because no matter how good the fishing was, I couldn't shake the feeling that there might be even better fishing just a little further upstream. This drive to keep exploring has shown me where the elusive brook trout begin to dominate a stream, and where secretive browns hold sway.

However, the truly important things I have learned about fishing these difficult streams have come from other fishermen. I have been blessed to meet a legion of talented fishermen that grew up fishing these streams. They learned how the skittish trout of the Smokies can be caught with a fly rod from their fathers and grandfathers. My quick progress and success in the Smokies has come from standing on the shoulders of those who came before me. Now, I would like to offer you the opportunity to learn the same techniques that I have been shown so that you may share in the same success that I have experienced.

Nearly every time I go fishing I see fishermen making the same mistakes. Some fishermen have a low opinion of streams in the Smokies because the trout here, particulary the large ones, are not very cooperative. Techniques used on tailwaters and Western rivers are not as effective on the freestone streams of the Southern Appalachians. Once a fisherman cracks the code, however, these streams can be as rewarding as streams anywhere. Their inherent natural beauty and solitude often make up for the relatively small size of the average fish. Size is relative, though, and you may be surprised at how many decently sized trout inhabit creeks traversed with a few short hops.

I spent over six years as a guide and fly shop manager in Townsend, Tennessee. Every day the same questions were asked and I hear the same problems time and again. Many of these questions are asked by beginners but many are asked by seasoned fishermen. Trout fishing in the Smokies is not difficult, only a little different from the way it's done in other parts of the country. I have attempted to answer the most common questions I have heard over the years: Where can I fish for a few hours and be back for dinner? Where can I catch a brookie? Where can I go to get away from the crowds? and of course ...What're they hittin' on? Some fishermen may not be interested in fishing near the road, and others may not have the time or desire to hike into back-country streams. Some fishermen like to camp. I have also noted that many fishermen like to target particular species. We all have our own reasons for fishing.

Now I invite you to see why those of us who fly fish in East Tennessee and Western North Carolina are such fanatics. Yes, we travel to fish in other places, but we have yet to find waters that are as challenging or any more beautiful.

How to Use this Book

The chapters in the first section of this book are intended to improve your fishing experience in the Great Smoky Mountains National Park. The information in these chapters will be valuable for freestone streams throughout the Southern Appalachian region. None of this information should steer you wrong in any trout fishing situation. Many of the methods and tactics described have proven extremely successful in the Rockies, and in the Northeast as well as in the Southeast. I know of one fisherman who had a wildly successful trip to New Zealand telling me he fished those rivers as if he was at home on Little River.

The chapters of the book dedicated to stream descriptions should give you a fair idea of what to expect. But there are a number of streams that have been omitted because most of them are currently closed to fishing in order to protect and research native brook trout populations. The locations of closed streams may be found on the maps at the beginning of each chapter. Some locations have been described in order to keep you from wandering into an illegal situation.

Streams have been grouped by their locality to the nearest accomodations adjacent to the park. This will allow you to quickly identify the most accessible streams in the area you are visiting.

There are plenty of roadside fishing opportunities in the Smokies, but most of the water will require hikes of some distance. You should get a detailed trail map if you intend to hike to any back-country locations. Only the most popular trails that allow fishing access are shown in this book. Detailed maps will prove valuable for travel in the back country.

Icons placed with stream names will allow you to quickly decide if a particular stream has attributes that suit your interests. Those anglers with limited time will be most interested in streams that feature the automobile icon. Someone interested in a remote fishing experience will probably seek out streams that only feature the hiking boots and tent icons. Remember though that the icons are only generalizations. Full details are given in each stream description. Often times, several fish species are shown with the icons. All of these are not usually present throughout the stream, but the detailed descriptions will give you a good idea of where each species is most likely to be found.

 Rainbow trout are present and likely to be caught

 Brown trout are present and likely to be caught

 Brook trout are present and likely to be caught

 Smallmouth and rock bass are present and likely to be caught

 Boat access at the mouth of the creek is an option to reach waters within the park's boundaries.

 A significant portion of the stream may be fished in close proximity to your car.

 The stream has areas that will require at least a minimum hike to reach.

 The stream is within easy reach of a developed campground in the park.

 Primitive backcountry campsites are available on the stream.

 Horses are allowed on the stream. Check detailed maps for areas where horses may be prohibited.

Trout Streams of the Great Smoky Mountains

The streams of the Great Smoky Mountains differ greatly from trout streams in other parts of the country. There are several factors that make streams in Southern Appalachia unique in the world of trout fishing. Weather, geology, geographic location, entomology, native plant life, and fisheries management policies have combined into a daunting obstacle for fishermen to overcome. Many fishermen find that their first experiences in the Smokies can be frustrating. Most seem to agree, however, that the problems they overcome in the Smokies make fishing in other locations seem easier.

The Smoky Mountains are among the oldest mountains in the world. The rocks here are so old that they do not even contain fossils. They predate life on earth. You will notice that most of the rocks are rounded. Sharp edges are uncommon. Most jagged rocks are found in streams along roads where construction shaped the rocks, not the slow wear of time. The mountains were once far taller than they are today. They have been beaten down by

the elements and are only a shadow of what they were hundreds of millions of years ago. Since the mountains are so old and worn away, there is very little nutrition left in them to seep into the streams. The lack of algae and aquatic plants, like watercress, best indicate less than optimal growing conditions. There is very little algae on the rocks and aquatic vegetation is almost negligible. The lack of basic mineral building blocks inhibits the growth of aquatic plants and insects. This essentially limits the amount of trout food in the streams, and if trout food is limited, so is the size of the trout. The Smokies are located close to the extreme southern range of trout in the eastern United States.

Hot, dry summers can put a lot of stress on trout in low elevation streams. This does not usually last more than a few weeks during the summer, but it can severely limit the growth of trout. Trout are cold-blooded animals and their metabolism is governed by the temperature of the water. As the water warms, their metabolism increases

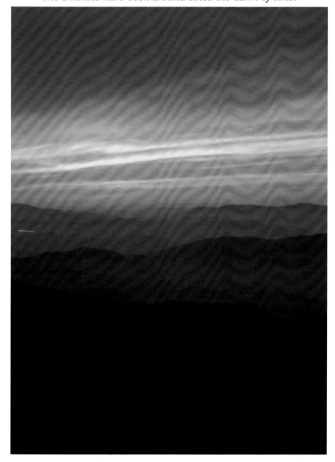

The Smokies have been around since the dawn of time.

High water is a common occurence that usually subsides within 24 hours.

along with their need for food. During periods of warm water, trout may have trouble finding enough food to maintain their body weight, let alone grow. Often times trout will be dormant during the hottest times of the day and only feed when the water is cooler, like early morning and late evening. This allows them to move about when their metabolism is a bit slower and the food they take in has a chance of making up for the energy expended.

As hot as summers might be for trout in the lower elevations, winters can be equally cold in small headwater streams. Ice and snow are common streamside sights in the winter, and water temperatures may not reach forty degrees for several months. To put it another way, trout are only a few degrees away from a block of ice in the winter. Extremely low temperatures will put any cold-blooded animal, like trout, in a catatonic state. Fishing in the winter can be difficult simply because fish are often too sluggish to feed regularly.

The flow of streams in the Smokies is completely controlled by rainfall. The Smoky Mountains are one of the wettest places in North America, receiving annual rainfall amounts comparable to the Amazon basin. The highest elevations can annually receive as much as 100 inches of rainfall. Since there are no dams that release water to control the stream flow, the water in the streams comes from

Golden stoneflies are found in the well oxygenated waters of the Smokies. It is common to find husks like these on the streams throughout the summer.

ground water. This means that the wetter the weather is, the more water there will be in the streams. Conversely, the drier the weather, the less water there is in the streams. Creeks in the Smokies undergo dynamic changes over the course of a year. Large streams, like Little River, may have an average flow of around 200-400 cubic feet per second, but it can decrease to 50 cubic feet per second or less during the driest times like August and September.

Rapids like this hold good numbers of fish in low to moderate flows. During high water there will not be many places to hold.

However, there may have been a day in March or April when the flow was over 10,000 cubic feet per second. Extremely high flows may happen relatively suddenly, but will usually ebb in a short time. Both high and low flows place limitations on trout habitat. Low flows shrink the size of the river, making good-sized pools with shelter and adequate food into prime real estate. High flows present the same problems, but valuable holding lies in low water may be too swift during floods. Large eddies and pools with structure to break the current become the places trout must find to survive.

Aquatic insects, also known as trout food, flourish in the waters of the Great Smokies. But they can influence fly fishermen differently here than in rivers elsewhere. The diversity of aquatic insects here is among the highest anywhere. Yet, among the tremendous variety of insects to be found, there are relatively few individuals of most species. This can prevent the fly fisherman from relying on one fly to make his day throughout the season. Spring creeks in Pennsylvannia and the tailwaters of Arkansas are flush with sow bugs that are eaten by trout every day of the year. Large rivers in the Rocky Mountains support large populations of stoneflies that are teeming on the river bottom all year long. Trout in the Smokies are rarely so single minded about food, though. There are several reliable hatches throughout the season, but even then,

exact fly imitations are not required to entice a strike. While many fishermen are sometimes frustrated by the lack of a sure thing, local fishermen look at it differently. They will often fish flies that are somewhat generic, representing any of a variety of insects. The bottom line is that the exact fly is far less important than its presentation.

The Southern Appalachian region is botanically rich because of its varied habitat and abundant rainfall. The shade provided by the many trees and shrubs keeps the water cool enough to support trout throughout the year. Many of these trees can test the skills and patience of a fly caster though, because most creeks can be described as tunnels through the brush. Short casts become a necessity in many places, and this forces fishermen to stalk every pool and pocket carefully so that he can approach close enough to make a cast that won't snag surrounding limbs and bushes. This is the signature Smoky Mountain flyfishing experience.

Streamside vegetation, and overhanging limbs, make long casts difficult at best. Every yard a fly is cast will send it past several potential snags. The need for short casts influences much of what a fisherman must do. Short casts make long leaders ineffective for all but the best fly casters. Even on the larger streams, it is rare to spot a fly caster with a leader over nine-feet long. Seven-and-a-half foot leaders are the norm for fishing pocket waters and small

Just getting your fly to the water is often the most difficult part of fishing the Smokies.

streams. When fishing the tightest streams, you might do well to shorten your leader to three or four feet. This close-in type of fishing demands that fishermen not stand out against the background. Most deer hunters are many yards from their quarry when they take a shot and camouflage is considered paramount. Smoky Mountain fly fishermen are usually less than 20 feet from a trout, so they take what they wear seriously, always avoiding bright colors.

The last factor that makes fishing in the park difficult has nothing to do with how nature has shaped the area, but how the streams are managed. Park streams are managed as wild trout streams. Trout are not stocked in these waters. Trout populations are controlled by the whim of Mother Nature. This is good for native and wild trout populations, but can spell trouble for fishermen not accustomed to trout with a savvy survival sense. Any fisherman that spends a lot of time casting to stocked trout will notice the difference. Eight-inch trout are tougher to fool here than most 14-inch trout in stocked rivers. Contrary to what most fishermen believe, they have little influence on Smoky Mountain trout populations. The biggest reason is because the trout are pretty hard to catch. Research by fisheries biologists in the park shows that only about ten percent of the trout population is ever effected in any given year by

Even the smallest streams in the Smokies are full of trout this size.

fishermen. Nearly 30 percent of the population dies every year through natural attrition. Droughts, floods, predation, and the amount of food in the stream have a far greater effect on trout than fishermen.

A catastrophic flood ravaged nearly all of the streams in the Southern Appalachians during the spring of 1994. Record flows were measured. The gauge on Little River read over 30,000 cubic feet per second before it washed out. Later that year, park biologists estimated that about half of the trout population was depleted by the flood waters. However, catch rates for fishermen were the same as they had been in previous years. This proved that there are usually more trout in the streams than the number fishermen catch. Another interesting thing to note is that larger fish turned up over the next couple of years. The aquatic insects, or food base, was not effected as much and it quickly returned to normal. This meant that the same amount of food in the streams had to feed fewer fish. The trout that survived the flood had more food to eat than during normal years and more fish grew larger as a result.

During a normal year, the largest segment of the trout population is composed of juveniles less than six inches. This accounts for a little more than half of the trout in the Smokies. Close to one-third of the trout population in an average-sized stream is between six to eight inches in length. That leaves about fifteen percent of the population larger than eight inches with only about five percent or less larger than 12 inches. However, don't be discouraged. Populations are so large that even small percentages translate into a decent number of good-sized fish. Most medium-sized streams have trout populations that are over 2,000 trout per mile. If a stream only has a five percent population of trout over 12 inches, that still leaves 100 trout per mile at least that large, but streams with good populations of brown trout will have more large fish than streams composed exclusively of rainbow or brook trout. Streams devoid of browns are far less likely to have appreciable numbers of trout over 12 inches.

Park biologists track trout populations

Gamefish of the Smokies

There are three species of trout in Great Smoky Mountains National Park: brook, rainbow, and brown trout. While all three are found in park waters, it is rare to find all three in the same place due to their different habitat preferences. Many of the best fishermen in the park can predict what species of trout will take their fly simply by where in a pool or run the fly was cast. Familiarity with each kind of favored habitat will lead to success, but always remember that there are several factors which will influence where each trout species will be found.

The brook trout is the only native trout found in the park, or the southeastern United States for that matter. Commonly referred to as a trout, and locally known as the "spec," the brookie is actually a member of the char family. The most recognizable feature of char that differentiates them from trout is their markings. Trout generally have dark spots against a lighter background , while char have light markings against a dark background.

Char are actually an arctic fish so it is quite interesting how they arrived in the southeastern United States. The last great ice age buried nearly all of what is north of Louisville, Kentucky under thick sheets of ice, and it was impossible for anything, especially fish, to maintain an existence in an environment composed of solid ice. Plant and animal species migrated south where the climate was less harsh. Tennessee and North Carolina were the ice age equivalent of today's northern Canada, but as the climate warmed and the ice sheets retreated, many northern species retreated with them. Yet, many plants and animals retreated up in elevation rather than in latitude. This marooned many northern plant and animal species in the high elevations of the Smokies where the climate is similar to Labrador, Canada.

Recent research has shown that all brookies south of the New River watershed in Virginia are genetically different than brookies to the north. This geographic isolation from other brook trout populations has caused southern brook trout to evolve separately from their northern cousins. The outward differences between the two populations are slight. Southern fish are more brightly colored with more red spots and are generally smaller fish. However, research shows that these two strains of fish are genetically further apart than the many strains of cutthroat trout in the West.

The cold, clear streams sheltered by towering trees were an idyllic home for brookies. The forest canopy kept sunlight from the streams and prevented the water temperature from creeping up. The very trees that guaranteed the brookies' survival in the Smokies though nearly brought about their destruction. Massive stands of virgin timber brought logging operations into the Southern Appalachians during the late 1800s and early 1900s. During an era of fron-

tier conquering, environmental concerns were nonexistent. The primeval forests of the Smokies soon became a moonscape. Waters warmed, and the lack of ground cover sent tremendous loads of silt into the streams. Many of the streams became too warm to sustain fish with an arctic heritage. Silt buried gravel that was essential for brookies to successfully lay their eggs. Only the highest elevations held brookies; generally areas that were too rugged to log. The scene was now set for the next trout to enter the Smokies.

In an effort to restore fish to the streams, rainbow trout were imported from their native West Coast in order to be released in the Smokies. Many assumed that the brookies would eventually rebound as the forests recovered, but the rainbows grew faster and were very aggressive in their movement upstream. The brook trout never regained their territory, losing to the invading rainbows.

The few places that became secure for the native specs were those streams that had waterfall barriers that rainbows could not overcome. Most people are surprised at what it takes to keep trout from advancing upstream. Biologists in the Smokies have found that if a waterfall is less than seven- or eight-feet tall, trout can usually get over it. Fortunately, there are enough high waterfalls in the park to keep rainbows from invading all native brook trout waters. The situation seemed to become dire enough that the park service closed most of the brook trout streams in 1975 and made it illegal to keep any. There was a reversal in 2002 and several streams were reopened. Several other streams that weren't closed had a regulation change that allowed for a fisherman to keep up to five brookies at least seven inches long. These streams will be monitored and if populations remain stable there is a good chance that all the streams in the park may be opened to fishing for brook trout.

Native Southern Appalachian brook trout have exceptionally bright coloration. This is a larger than average catch.

Recent stream population surveys are showing that brook trout are finally beginning to colonize further downstream in some streams, coexisting with rainbows. There is no way of knowing if this trend is permanent or only temporary. Restoration efforts by the national park service are also getting specs back in a few streams where they were historically found.

Brook trout typically prefer the calmer waters of the streams where they are most frequently found. While they may be found in riffles, they are more at home in eddies and calm pockets. Since many of the streams with exclusive brook trout populations are closed to fishing, rainbows may also be present where brook trout fishing is available. Carefully placing your fly in the calmer waters will often tempt brookies while rainbows keep to the main currents. Many of the streams where brookies are found are very small though, and require some skill in casting because the brush is so tight.

Rainbows are the most abundant game fish in the Smokies. Found in all major watersheds they are usually the fish that anglers catch most often. Rainbows are generally small in the Smokies, averaging five to seven inches. A rainbow over nine inches is a good fish and one over 12 inches is extraordinary. Abrams Creek is probably the best stream to catch a better than average rainbow. The largest rainbow ever found in the park by biologists during a population survey was an 18-1/2-inch brute near the Abrams Falls trailhead in 1999. Many stocked rainbows from outside the park will migrate upstream and make the park their home. This is somewhat common in the lower reaches of streams that flow out of the park. These rainbows are usually above average in length and weight, and usually will not exhibit the "stream smarts" of the their wild counterparts. Occasionally large rainbows are caught in the streams that feed Fontana or Chilhowee Lake. These fish are fairly rare and only spend a brief amount of time in the stream before returning to their more comfortable existence in the lake.

Rainbows love swift currents and tumbling pocket waters. In fact, many anglers fish waters that are too slow to catch good numbers of rainbows, but rainbows always

Most rainbows caught in the Smokies will be between five and eight inches long.

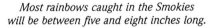

Smallmouth bass are often overlooked by fishermen in the Smokies. They are very common in most of the lower elevation streams.

come willingly to the dry fly. Combine this with their affinity for pocket water and you have the perfect dry-fly quarry. Bushy dry flies with a noticeable silhouette attract rainbows holding near heavy currents.

Brown trout are the newcomers to park waters. They are easily distinguished from other Smoky Mountain trout by their coloration and markings. They are generally yellow or gold with large red and dark brown spots that have haloes. Some older fishermen can remember when they weren't even present in waters where they are now common, yet browns were never officially stocked in park waters. Many of the populations started when fish swam upstream from stockings that occurred outside of the park. This, however, does not explain how browns ended up above barrier waterfalls like the Sinks on Little River. Undoubtedly, brown trout had some covert help getting to many of the areas they now call home.

The largest trout in the Smokies are browns. Surprisingly, a few will grow as large as their brethren in the fabled rivers of the American West or the spring creeks of Pennsylvania. Large browns are, without a doubt, the most cautious and skittish trout in the Smokies.

Browns prefer slower waters with plenty of cover from predators. For that reason, they are not usually the predominant game fish in the turbulent streams of the Smokies. Pools and slow runs will usually harbor more browns than stretches of pocket water, but browns found in pockets will usually be under boulders that shield them from currents, as well as overhead predators. But don't think that big boulders and logs are the only things they hide under because swirling foam in a pocket is often suitable cover for a feeding brown.

Browns are often willing to take a dry fly, but they may also be caught more reliably on nymphs or streamers. The reason is simple—if they are wedged under rocks and logs, they will not notice food on the surface. Nymphs drifted under rocks will often enter the lair of a hungry brown. Brown trout hiding under cover often use the same tactics as a backstreet mugger, waiting in the shadows for an unsuspecting victim to come along. Strikes on slowly retrieved streamers can be jarring.

Brown trout better than twelve inches long are common in the Smokies. However, because of their cautious nature they are not commonly caught.

Brown trout also tend to have more nocturnal habits than rainbows or brookies. Adapted to night time hunting, dusk and dawn can be the best times to catch a nice brown. Remember, though, that browns are still cold-blooded and they prefer warm daytime temperatures over cold overnight temperatures in the late autumn, winter, and early spring.

Bass are easily the most overlooked game fish in the Smokies. Smallmouth and redeye bass are both found in lower elevation park streams. But almost all that are caught are done so by accident since most fishermen are angling for trout. Besides, it is extremely rare to find a fisherman who is fishing for bass in the park.

Perhaps it is the bright coloration found on trout that place them higher on anglers' lists because it certainly isn't because bass are poor fighters, though stream smallmouth are generally smaller than their brethren found in lakes in the region. However, mountain stream currents, and the abundance of snags and boulders, seem to make them better fighters.

Smallmouth bass are native to the streams where they are foun, but they were probably more abundant before rainbow and brown trout were introduced. Little is known, but it is speculated that rainbow and brown trout—which are better suited to swift water—have out competed smallmouth for the same habitat.

Redeyes, also known as rock bass, are usually small. They are not native to park waters but are widespread throughout the region. They will take bluegill poppers, as well as conventional streamer and nymph patterns used for trout. They will take dry flies as well, but not with the same consistency.

Smallmouth can reach respectable sizes, especially in the larger streams where they are found. Some three- to five-pound specimens have been caught in Abrams Creek, yet more would probably be caught if more people were fishing for them. Bass are as sensitive to fishermen as trout. Many, however, don't look the part. I have often seen smallmouth bass watch me intently as I waded through streams. Not once have any of these fish shown an interest in my lure, though. While a smallmouth may not run and hide like a trout, that doesn't mean he's not on to your game.

Streamers and big nymphs are the most consistent bass getters. Dry flies can work—especially terrestrial patterns in the summer. Poppers can also work well and draw the most dramatic strikes.

Smallmouth and redeyes both like the same type of water as trout. However, they like to hide under boulders, logs, or lie deep to stay hidden; their habits are very similar to those of brown trout.

Smoky Mountain Fishing Methods

All too often I overhear fishermen saying that streams in the Smokies must be fished out or that our mountain streams just don't hold trout like larger tailwaters. While most of our fish are small when compared to tailwaters in the region, there is no shortage of them. Annual fisheries surveys conducted on Little River have determined that there are between 2,000 and 3,000 trout per mile, while other park streams boast comparable numbers. What most unsuccessful anglers fail to realize is that Smoky Mountain trout are among the most easily spooked trout anywhere.

You just can't be sneaky enough when fishing the Smokies. I've even heard one local fisherman joke that he tries not to slam his truck door when he arrives on the stream. The trout here dodge kingfishers, otters, herons, water snakes, and the occasional lunker brown trout every day of their lives. These predators fish for a living and have to be good to get a meal, and with such lethal neighbors, trout wedge themselves under the nearest rock at the first sign of trouble. A fly fisherman will have a tough time match-ing the consistent success of a kingfisher. In order to do so in the Smokies, fishermen must emulate the qualities of trout predators. The most important qualities are camouflage and a stealthy approach. These two factors will account for more trout than a box of meticulously tied trout flies. The point is to do everything you can to reduce evidence of your pres-ence. Remember, no matter how good your fly is, fish will not bite if they are under a rock fearing for their lives.

You can always pick the experienced Smoky Mountain fisherman out of a lineup by his clothing. Fishing shirts and vests are shades of green or brown, making them able to blend into the background. Hats are similarly colored. A few fishermen favor gray clothing when fishing the most boulder strewn streams. A white cap will always decrease your catch and a blaze-orange cap will mark you as a sure novice to trout and fishermen alike. Many fishermen will even go so far as to wear camouflage patterned clothing on the stream. Remember, the trout you spook may be the fish of a lifetime.

Wearing camouflage clothing is a good way to get closer to fish without spooking them. Getting close is a good way to get a good drift.

Casting from behind boulders or logs in the stream is a good way to conceal your presence from fish.

This is an experienced fisherman. Notice he is keeping a low profile. He is also not wading which would alert fish of his presence.

Stay low so that trout can't see you. The higher you are above the water, the more you will stand out to them. Fishing a pool from atop the tallest boulder in the stream is a sure way to spook every fish in sight. Some fishermen fish shallow water from a kneeling position to keep a low profile. Another advantage to staying low is that you can give yourself more overhead clearance for casting.

Wading spooks more fish than anything—except for clumsy wading. Move slowly so you don't telegraph ripples through a pool, or better yet, stay out of the water whenever possible. Sound actually transmits better in water than air, so splashing or kicking rocks in the stream bed is easily detected by a trout. Trout hear with the extremely sensitive lateral line that runs the length of their body, and sound made outside of the water is not transmitted through the water as well. For this reason, it makes sense to walk on the bank to get as close as possible to your target before wading the last few steps into position. Wading is best avoided in slow, flat pools because waves created by your movement will alert any fish in the pool of your presence.

Most fishermen do not consider their shadow when placing themselves in position to cast. However, a shadow cast on the water is one of the most obvious signs of danger to a fish because moving shadows on the water usually indicate an approaching predator or careless fisherman. Try to position yourself so that your shadow does not fall across a trout's lie. If you can't position yourself so that your shadow won't cast in the direction of the fish, stay back, and be sure to cast beyond your shadow but don't forget about the shadow of your fly line, either. The shadow of a false cast fly line can be pronounced on bright days.

Use natural cover to your advantage. If you have the opportunity to approach a pool by staying behind a boulder, do it. There will also be times when the pool or pocket you are casting to is several feet higher than the pool below it. Try casting from the lower pool into the higher pool if wading conditions permit. The plunge you are wading in will conceal any noises made by your feet. Also, if the pool you are casting into is level with your chest, you will be at a comparable level as if you had cast while lying on your stomach.

One of the best ways to sneak up on fish is to move and cast upstream because trout always position themselves facing into current. By moving upstream you will be coming at the fish from behind but, as with most rules, there is an exception to this. Not all water moves downstream. Some currents may flow sideways to the stream bed and water can sometimes swirl upstream in eddies.

You should move upstream, but be aware of currents that do not flow directly downstream. The more accurate way of stating the fact is to try to fish up current.

The most successful fishermen in the Smokies will rarely fish a spot for very long before moving on. Food is not as abundant for trout in the Smokies as it is for trout elsewhere. Most Smoky Mountain trout hate to see a potential meal get away and are pretty aggressive. Fishermen find that their most productive cast is their first cast because each cast after that has less of a chance of fooling a fish. As an insect drifts downstream, it never moves back upstream, floating through a run a second time. For that reason, hungry Appalachian trout will let few potential meals go by without an inspection. Besides, the longer you stand in a spot casting, the more conspicuous you become. Moving from one spot, to the next, also puts your fly in front of more trout. You will have far better results placing your fly in front of more unsuspecting trout, instead of giving one pool of trout a thorough education.

Many fishermen new to fishing freestone streams are surprised at how rough the water can be, yet still hold trout. One mistake that many fishermen make is to restrict their fishing only to deep, still pools. These big holes certainly hold fish, but are the toughest places to fool them. Trout in calm water can be very resolute in their feeding activities since the current will be slow. Because the water is placid, fish can see you, your line and tippet, and they can tell the difference between a Mustad and Tiemco hook. The only time a big hole will fish consistently though is during a good hatch when trout are feeding vigorously.

Pocket water, on the other hand, puts the advantage squarely in the hands of fishermen because trout holding there are usually feeding. Also, since the water is swifter, their decision time will often be less than a second. Many hungry trout will grab even questionable drifting objects, assuming they can be spit out if it isn't food. The turbulence of the water also makes your presence less obvious. A fisherman can't push a wake ahead of himself in a swift current. Tippet becomes virtually invisible, and even sloppy casting is less likely to disturb trout. Many fishermen believe that only small trout will be caught in pocket water, but some of the most coveted feeding stations are in sections of rough water so never overlook them.

❧ Adjusting Your Fishing Style ❧

Keeping a low profile and sneaking up on fish is a large part of the equation but there is still more to be done. The fly must be cast to a trout, and drifted naturally to draw a strike, but visiting fishermen—who are familiar with larger rivers—can have a tough time adjusting to Appalachian trout streams. I often hear visitors refer to Little River as tight or brushy and I immediately recognize that they are not local. Little River is one of the most open trout streams in all of Southern Appalachia, offering the casting space of all Montana compared to many other creeks. If a fisherman from Cosby, Tennessee says a stream has tight casting conditions, you can bet that just carrying a fly rod is an inconvenience.

The average cast made in the Smokies is a fairly short one. Even on larger streams most casts will be less than 20 feet and there are several reasons for this. To most casters, the obvious reason would be the thick vegetation since every foot your fly travels through the air sends it past that many more leaves and tree branches. The more practical reason, though, is that long casts will often have bad drifts. Currents are usually very irregular, and long casts covering three or more currents, pull your line and fly in as many directions. If a fly is not drifting naturally, few fish will strike because most insects drift helplessly with the current. This concept is not unique to the Smokies, it's just a little trickier to achieve at times. Suitable spots to drop a fly may only accommodate the fly and a foot or so of tippet. In order to get a good drift, your fly line should rarely touch the water in stretches of rough pocket water.

After shortening your cast, you may need to adjust the way that you cast your rod. Resident Smoky Mountain fishermen stick out like sore thumbs when they travel to East Tennessee's tailwaters. Their habitual sidearm cast is as recognizable as their Southern good-old-boy accents. Yet, the sidearm casts just make good sense when fishing the tree-lined creeks of the Smokies. They keep your fly down and out of overhanging limbs. But always remember to keep false casting to a minimum. The longer a fly is in the air, the less time it spends on the water drifting over fish. More importantly, though, the more false casts you make, the more likely you are to hang up in tree limbs.

Southern Appalachian fly casters are also exceptionally good roll casters since they have to employ this technique more than fishermen in other parts of the country.

Pocket water like this can often be the most productive water in the stream. However, short casts are necessary in order to get a good drift.

A good roll caster can have his back to the thorniest brush on the creek and his fly will never come close to getting hung up in it. Practice your roll casting before you come. You'll be glad you did.

❧ Gear Considerations ❧

When visiting fishermen first see our streams, they often assume that we fish extremely short rods. In many of the smallest and brushiest streams we do, but when fishing the most popular streams, we often use the same size rods used on large tailwaters. An eight-foot, four-weight rod is probably the most universal rod for the Smokies. If you expect to confine your fishing to #14 dry flies or smaller, you may want to consider a lighter rod. Many nymph fishers prefer five- or even six-weight rods. These rods can lob the heavy flies required to reach bottom in turbulent water.

More important than the weight of your rod is its length. Longer rods are often easier to work with than short ones. Short casts in pocket water are easier to control with a long rod and mending line. Simply keeping it off of the water is easier to achieve as well. Large streams—such as Abrams Creek, Little River, and the Oconaluftee—can easily accommodate nine-foot rods. Medium-size streams are best for rods seven-and-a-half feet to eight-and-a-half-feet long. The smallest streams—like Collins and Jakes creeks—are best fished with rods less than eight-feet long.

Fly lines are often overlooked but their qualities can be a great asset or liability. Never use a distance taper to fish in the Smokies since these lines are usually lighter in the first thirty feet and have heavy bellies. The problem is that you will have very few opportunities for a cast that lets you enjoy the benefits of the line. Double-taper and weight-forward lines are both adequate, and most fly fishers have a preference for one over the other. Brightly colored lines can help someone learning how to fish in the swift water environment because their high visibility makes it easy to track their course and anticipate drag. However, experienced Smoky Mountain fly fishers shun brightly colored lines. Why dress in camouflage clothing if you plan to zip a neon orange line over the fish? Gray and olive fly lines are the favorite colors. Most novices find these lines tough to see though and should avoid them. Visible shades of green and tan are good colors that are easy to see, but do not have a glow that trout can see before you even make a cast.

Leader size is also important to consider. There is absolutely no reason to fish an eighteen-foot, 7X leader in the Smokies. The average leader on the popular streams will be nine-feet, 5X. If you are fishing smaller streams, or making short casts in pocket water, a seven-and-a-half foot, 5X may be the most appropriate. Some of the tightest streams may require that you cut your leader down to around three feet. Remember, a 12-foot leader is almost worthless when you're casting fifteen feet or less. Choose a leader length that allows you to cast accurately. Also, the generally swift nature of the water minimizes the need for extremely fine tippets. Many successful nymph fishermen routinely use 3X in the Smokies.

❧ Creative Fly Casting ❧

Fly fishing the Smokies often requires that an angler stop and look around before making a cast. Often times, the back cast is more difficult than the actual cast to a trout because you may find yourself aiming a back cast through gaps in the brush. Sometimes a roll cast is more efficient than a conventional cast. There are times, though, when a roll cast just won't fit the situation. The wide, arching loop of a roll cast will often snag brush above the desired target. This is a situation that calls for some creative fly casting.

An easy solution to this problem is to simply turn around and make your back cast the cast to the trout. By aiming your naturally more accurate forward cast at the gap in the brush, you should be able to avoid any entanglements. Simply stopping your back cast, allowing it to fall to the water, will hopefully put it in front of a willing trout.

The bow and arrow cast is valuable in truly tight situations. This cast can be difficult to master, but the good news is that no true fly casting skill is required. While holding the tippet between the thumb and forefinger of your line hand, draw it back so it pulls the rod tip back. You must grip the fly line against the cork grip with your rod hand. Aim and release. There is no back cast to hang up behind you, and there is a much tighter loop than provided by a roll cast. A fisherman that is skilled with this cast can tackle the tightest streams in the Smokies. However, this is a good cast to practice in the open without a fly on the leader, but once you get the timing down, try it with a fly. I can assure you, though, you will stick yourself with the hook at least a few times so be sure to use barbless hooks. (If you listen closely, you may hear the voice of experience.)

A short rod and a bow and arrow cast are your most valuable tools when fishing small streams and tight cover.

Trout Fishing Seasons in the Smoky Mountains

The climate of the Smokies is an important consideration for trout fishermen since the Smoky Mountains are close to the southern-most limit for trout in the eastern United States. This has both good and bad effects. The geographic location of the Smokies accounts for somewhat mild temperatures most of the year, but there are a few weeks every winter with bitter weather and some oppressively hot days during the summer as well. However, the Smokies have one of the friendliest year-round climates for fishermen.

Winter rarely sets in before mid-December in Southern Appalachia, with autumn weather often lingering close to Christmas. January and February can be bitter as snow often blankets the highest peaks and ridges throughout this period. Without a doubt, this is the least likely time of the year to find another fisherman in your favorite pool. Those other fishermen may be smarter than you are, though, staying warm, tying flies in front of a ball game while you're out wading in ice-cold water, catching few (if any) trout. In spite of cold weather, fishing during the winter months can be productive, particularly if you are mindful of several factors.

Mild days should produce more trout than record cold days, but fishing will be best after several days of mild weather because this gives the water a chance to warm a few degrees. Fish are cold-blooded and their activities are dictated entirely by the temperature of the water—temperatures above 40 degrees are more productive than temperatures in the thirties. The best you can hope for in the winter will be water temperatures in the neighborhood of 45 degrees. Areas that receive sunlight are good bets during the winter months, with lower elevation streams often flowing through more open coves and valleys. This means that they will receive more sunlight to warm the water. Streams in deep, narrow valleys or gorges may get less than an hour of direct sunlight, if any, in a day. Since this shade prevents snow from melting, areas are kept in a deep-freeze for days, or even weeks, after a snowstorm.

Spring offers the best time of year to consistently catch nice trout on dry flies. This brown took a Quill Gordon.

Pink Ladyslippers and Showy Orchis flower during the height of the spring hatches.

Water temperatures in these areas are usually lower than they are downstream.

There is no point getting out on the stream at daylight in the winter because water temperatures will be at their warmest in the middle of the day, but once the sun gets off of the water, temperatures begin to fall. The best fishing will be had from about 11 AM until about 3 PM, but some spots may have prime sun exposure early, or even late in the day, not necessarily at midday. Fishing on especially cold days can mean chasing the sunny spots, particularly for anyone hoping to hook a trout with a dry fly.

Water is at its clearest during the winter, but be sure to approach a pool or run carefully when it is in full sunlight. Never let your shadow cast in the direction you plan to fish. Even though trout have a slow metabolism in the cold water, they will still spook or get a case of lockjaw if they are alerted to your presence.

Low water temperatures translate into sluggish trout. The best way to catch a lethargic trout is to get your fly as close as possible, not making him work to eat it. This usually means fishing nymphs deep. Insects will emerge through the winter, but most trout will choose to remain in a comfortable lie on the bottom, only picking off nymphs that drift in close proximity to them. Big stonefly patterns are standard wintertime fare, but don't neglect smaller nymphs. Small dun caddis, blue wing olive mayflies, tiny black stoneflies, and midges are the most common wintertime insect hatches. The nymphs, or pupae of these insects, are active and the most common food items trout see. A large stonefly nymph fished in tandem with a smaller Pheasant Tail or Hare's Ear Nymph is a good way to cover your bases. The larger nymph may stir a trout to move and strike, but the smaller nymph may be more representative of what trout have been eating and are expecting. Don't be shy though about applying weight to your leader because if your fly is not ticking bottom, there's a good chance you won't get any strikes.

If you're a dry fly purist, don't despair. There are opportunities to catch trout on a dry fly. Larger pools will often have a few fish waiting for emergences of caddis, blue wing olives, or midges. This is usually for about one to two hours during the middle of the day. If you have a tough time fooling risers in smooth water, try fishing similar patterns in shallow pocket water. You may find that you can have more success than you expected fishing water two-feet deep or less. Just be sure to fish calmer pockets where sluggish fish might feel at home.

Spring comes relatively early to the Southern Appalachians. Many wildflowers will begin to bloom by the first days of March. Significant mayfly hatches may also begin to take wing by mid-March. Quill Gordon and Blue Quill mayflies will begin to hatch once water temperatures hover near 50 degrees for several days. Once a stream has begun to warm, the mayfly nymphs begin to metamorphasize. They begin to develop and have no choice but to hatch. Some of the best fishing to be had

*A Light Cahill mayfly completes its life cycle
by laying eggs on the water before dying.*

can occur during raw days after a mild spell of weather. Many mayflies hatch during warm, springlike days. But many also hatch when the weather is less than ideal for them to fly away before drifting over an alert trout. Cool weather makes it extremely hard for mayflies to get enough strength in their wings to fly away before being eaten.

Quill Gordons get most of the recognition from fishermen for great dry fly fishing. Most of these clumsy mayflies will be a #12, with a few as large as #10, but don't overlook the diminutive Blue Quill. These smaller mayflies hatch at about the same time as Quill Gordons, but in much greater numbers. The tremendous numbers of hatching Blue Quills get the trout looking to the surface for a reliable meal after several months of foraging for drifting nymphs. These size 18 to 20, dark-colored mayflies are often referred to as blue wing olives but they are not Baetis as blue wing olives are. These insects will hatch simultaneously, though, and considering the smaller size and dark color of these mayflies, it is doubtful that trout bother to distinguish between the two. Most of what a rising trout eats during the early season will not be Quill Gordons. Yet, when one of these large mayflies drifts down the river, flopping helplessly in an attempt to gain flight, it is usually just too much for any trout to resist. These hatches begin as early as 11 AM and can last as late as 5 PM. The most reliable hours and intense periods of the hatch are between 1 to 3 PM. Since there are both small and large insects hatching, you can do reasonably well with any dark-colored mayfly imitation in sizes 12 to 18. If you keep your eyes open and match the size of the fly to what's on the water you should do extremely well.

Rainbow trout spawn during this period, but it shouldn't affect your fishing. Rainbows are plentiful enough, and spawning habitat is widespread enough, that fish don't seem to take on any migrations. Besides, if the opportunity becomes available, spawning rainbows also seem to take time out to feed.

Water levels during the spring can be high, but don't let this intimidate you. Spring downpours may raise the streams to astounding levels in just a few hours, but it is rare for this condition to last for long. Fish can almost always be found when the water clears, no matter what the level is, yet many fishermen regard potentially ideal stream conditions as being too high. This is usually because wading can be difficult and even dangerous due to water levels. Far too much energy is wasted on wading, though. Casting from banks will be far more productive. Large pools may have eddies where it is safe to get in up to your ankles, but it is important to remember that anywhere the water is calm enough for you to wade, it is also calm enough for trout to take shelter. High water is a relatively common occurrence that trout cope with and enjoy far more than most fishermen do. If you take your time, you will notice that roll casts can be made from the banks in many spots. Carefully wading in shallow spots can give you plenty of room to fish productive runs and pockets. True, you can't fish the whole stream when the water is high. However, the careful caster should be able to get a fly on at least thirty percent of the water in the stream.

As spring days begin to grow longer and the water warms, good fishing can be had well into the evening. Hatches will begin to lengthen and more insects will begin to appear. March Browns and Hendricksons will join the quills, eventually replacing them as the season progresses. Light Cahill mayflies and small yellow stoneflies, known as Yellow Sallies, will begin to hatch as April turns into May. These hatches are best in the evening and can coincide with egg-laying flights. The Little Yellow Stonefly, or Yellow Sally as it is commonly called, can be one of the best hatches of the year. Without a doubt, this is the most prolific insect hatch that fishermen see on streams in Southern Appalachia. Thousands may be in the air for a few

Rhododendrons bloom along the streams in June and July.

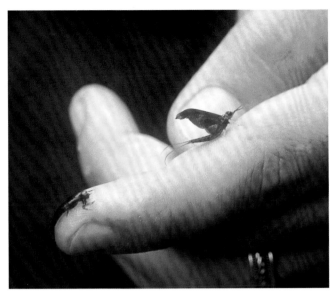

Isoncychia mayflies, also known as Mahogany Duns hatch sporadically through summer and early fall.

minutes, most evenings, from late April through May. This can be frustrating, though. There are times trout will not rise in spite of the stoneflies buzzing about. This is because stonefly nymphs crawl out of the water onto rocks or riverbanks before shedding their nymph husks to become adults. Unless conditions are windy, very few adults will fall to the water to become prey for trout. Fishing a nymph or wet fly that represents these insects is often more productive than a dry fly during these emergences. Tellico Nymphs and the venerable Yellarhammer are among the best flies to tie on.

The dry fly fisherman should keep looking, though, because after several nights of hatching, stoneflies will mate and females will return to the water to lay eggs. This will be seen as the Sallies bounce on the surface of the water to dislodge their eggs. Trout will often strike viciously as the stoneflies try to propagate their species. As the eggs are layed, most of the females will die, exhausted on the water, as the trout feast. This is the best time to fish a Yellow Sally dry fly, but if all the Sallies you see are only flying upwards, a nymph may do better than a dry. If most of the flies are bouncing on the water, the dry fly should produce well.

Afternoon thunderstorms begin to appear in May and will continue throughout the summer. It is amazing how quickly these storms can build, drop buckets of rain, and then diminish. Most of these storms will not last more than an hour and may only affect rather small areas. It is quite common for lightning to crack overhead while thunder echoes off the mountainsides, but the rain never comes. Conversely, it is also common for you to hear only the slightest thunder clap but the creek will rise over a foot in five minutes. These thunderstorms are a way of life in the Smokies where trout have come to expect the treats that rising water brings. Thunderstorms also cool water temperatures during the heat of the summer, and as long as there is not a significant flash flood, fishing can be exceptional after a brief storm.

By June, daytime heat will warm the water, slowing fishing during the day. As water temperatures increase, the metabolism of fish in the stream will also increase. A trout's metabolism can get so high at that time chasing food in the currents will burn more energy than it can obtain. For this reason, trout will often lie on the bottom in a place where they can easily rest without expending much energy and wait to feed when the water cools in the evening. Streams in the higher elevations will have cooler temperatures than larger, low elevations streams. The larger streams will fish best early in the morning, late in the evening, or on rainy days when heat isn't a factor.

There are no really reliable hatches through the summer, so terrestrials are the only insects fish are sure to see everyday. Stoneflies and Isonychia mayflies will hatch on a sporadic basis through the summer months, with most of the large stoneflies usually hatching during the middle of the night. Their empty nymph husks can be found on river rocks, but no one ever seems to see them hatch. Stonefly nymphs work well in pocket water and deep runs. Stimulators and large Elk Hair Caddis are good adult stonefly imitations that can work with exceptional results. Isonychias, also known as Mahogany Duns, usually hatch in the evening. They hatch the same way stoneflies do, crawling out of the water onto rocks to shed their nymph exoskeleton, then flying to the trees. As a result, they are usually available to trout while they are still nymphs swimming to the bank. Pheasant Tail, Zug Bug, and Prince Nymphs in a size 12 are all imitations that work well.

Grasshoppers, crickets, beetles, ants, and inchworms are all found along stream banks in the summer. Many have the misfortune of falling into streams, becoming meals for hungry trout. Those trout seeking shelter from the heat, and swifter currents, will hold under the shade of tree limbs or bushes near the bank. Yet, not only do they find shade and shelter. Terrestrial insects are likely to fall from overhanging limbs into their laps. Terrestrial patterns can be particularly productive throughout the summer and into the autumn.

The presence of large stoneflies makes big nymphs productive most of the year in the Smokies.

Leave the waders at home during the summer and you'll be far more comfortable. Water temperatures are usually in the mid to high 60's.

Summer fishing can be only second in difficulty to mid-winter fishing. Stream flows are often low, trout are less than enthusiastic about feeding, and crowds are at a maximum. Swimmers and tubers will often outnumber fishermen on roadside streams. These streams are best fished early and late to avoid crowds. However, one positive effect is that many trout seem to grow accustomed to people in the most popular swimming holes. For this reason, trout in these spots are not at all skittish through the summer. I have even caught trout out of pools while people were swimming, though I often wonder if overweight swimmers in tight spandex swimsuits cause trout to lose their appetites.

Waders can often be too warm to bother with and most fishermen just wear felt-soled boots to wade in. This can be a good time of year to hike in to streams that are off the beaten path. There are no waders to pack, temperatures are usually cooler in the back country, and trout in these locales are often a bit more cooperative. Streams are often smaller in the higher elevations, but the fast action of naive, eager trout allows many fishermen to catch them in spite of tighter casting conditions.

By late September temperatures will begin to cool. The respite from the heat will energize the fish and they will start to feed regularly throughout the day. The best fly patterns are usually smaller than they are in the spring and summer. Midges, as well as small mayflies and caddis, are predominant foods available with terrestrials still falling in the streams. The water is usually very low and clear in the autumn so the margin for error is very slim. While larger attractor patterns will still catch some trout in rougher water, size 18 Blue Wing Olive Parachutes and Comparaduns, as well as midge patterns, will fool far more fish in pools and long glides. Basic nymph patterns can often be more productive than dry flies during the coolest conditions. You may also try dropping a very small midge pattern off of a more conventionally sized dry fly on sunny days. Tailwater style midge pupa do very well in the fall, but are often not worth the trouble of fishing alone if a good number of trout will still eat a size 16 dry fly. Try dropping a size 20 or 22 midge pupa off of your dry fly and you may be surprised how many trout prefer it.

In spite of the sometimes tough fishing conditions, this is one of the best times of year to plan a trip. Hatches of blue wing olives and cinammon caddis can be excellent, and the weather is usually cool and dry. The fall colors which peak in mid- to late October are among the brightest to be found. The catching may not always be prime, but the memory of fishing these pristine streams, painted in the hues of autumn, is one to treasure.

Falling leaves can be a nuisance to fishermen, tumbling in the currents as well as on the breeze. Expect to hook plenty of leaves, especially if you are nymph or streamer fishing. The leaves will actually stain the water as they create a Smoky Mountain hardwood leaf tea. I know some fishermen that put up their gear once the leaves start falling, but I find this to be entirely unreasonable because in fact, the falling leaves may distract the trout and allow you to sneak up without being noticed.

Brook and brown trout can be found spawning in the fall, usually starting in October and carrying on through November. Just like the leaves on the trees, they will be wearing their most brilliant colors of the year. The largest browns in the streams will come out to play, and although they are no easier to fool or any less skittish, they will be out from whatever rock they've spent the year hiding under. Take care wading streams that are home to browns and brookies. Spawning trout lay their eggs in gravelly areas, usually in side currents or in the tails of pools. Wading through these areas can destroy a redd, which is a trout's nest of developing eggs.

December can be a fickle month, sometimes fair and sometimes frigid. If temperatures are agreeable, fishing can be exceptional. Spawned out brown trout come to a fly better now since they have to eat to make up for lost body weight. Small dun caddis usually hatch with a smattering of blue wing olives and midges to keep them company. This is often just enough for some trout to keep a watchful eye on the surface. While dry fly fishing can be productive in December, as well as on mild days throughout the winter, this is usually when nymph fishing begins in earnest. A box full of beadheads will serve you much better than a box of dry flies.

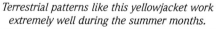

Terrestrial patterns like this yellowjacket work extremely well during the summer months.

While they are very pretty, autumn leaves make life hard on the fisherman.

Fishing for Larger Trout in the Smokies

Smoky Mountain streams should generally be regarded as small trout fisheries. The bulk of trout they contain will be nine inches or smaller. However, I am constantly amazed at how many large brown trout can be found in Southern Appalachia. My first experiences with some of these trout were by sheer accident. Occasionally I would spook one while wading, and on a few rare occasions, one would try to remove a smaller trout from the end of my line. A little bit of guidance, mixed with large doses of patience, and persistence have helped me catch more than my fair share of nice browns. Many fishermen have a poor understanding of what goes into hooking and catching a big brown trout in the Smokies. My intention is to separate fact from fiction and to give you the knowledge necessary to catch a memorable fish.

First and foremost, when fishing Smoky Mountain streams, remember that a "big" trout will almost always be a brown trout, but there are a few instances when this may not be the case. Run-up trout from one of the lakes surrounding the park may be found in some of the streams. However, this is not usually the case. Wild rainbows and brookies in park streams are usually under nine inches, with some rainbows approaching up to twelve. Abrams Creek is the only stream in the park that has any realistic chance, albeit slim, for a rainbow over 12 inches. If you want consistent opportunities at trout over 12 inches focus on streams with good populations of brown trout.

Most fly fishermen focus on dry fly fishing. This is, without a doubt, the most enjoyable way to fish. It is unrealistic though to fish only dry flies throughout the year and have consistent opportunities for nice browns. Spring is the best season for the dry fly fisherman to hook up with a good one. Water flows are usually ideal and there is usually enough food on the surface to keep them looking up. However, the best brown trout will usually be wedged under a rock or log, even when feeding, and this may not allow them to see a fly on the surface. Really large trout, 16 inches and larger, are masters of efficiency. Rising to eat flies on the surface is not as efficient as finding a comfortable lie on the bottom and having nymphs drift into their mouths. Streamers are overlooked almost entirely by many Smoky Mountain fishermen. Again, these flies should sink to where many of these toothy predators hide.

Most fishermen put their rod up and go home when it starts to rain. Fishing is a leisure activity and should be fun. While fishing in the rain can be miserable, it can also be phenomenal. Staying home on a rainy or overcast day is perhaps the biggest mistake a serious fisherman can make. Overcast or rainy days are undoubtedly the best ones for hooking into good fish. This piece of advice works well for

trout anywhere. There are no shadows for the fisherman to cast on the water, and no bright reflections from a wrist watch or guides on a rod. Many trout predators are not active when these conditions occur, and trout have evolved to take advantage of this. Besides, large browns are ambush predators, so they prefer to feed in low-light conditions.

One complaint I hear throughout the spring is that the water is too high to fish effectively. There are times when it can be hazardous because of flood waters, but the average springtime stream flow is usually ideal for catching trout of any species. Wading can be difficult when the banks are full, yet wading spooks more trout than it catches and should be kept to a minimum under any conditions. Trout will feed on emerging mayflies or caddis in high water that is clear and should rise well in these conditions. Higher stream flows are also the prime time to fish with nymphs or streamers. Be sure these flies sink well and get good drifts through prime lies.

Persistence and patience catch more big trout than well tied flies.

Wild rainbow trout this big are rare in the freestone streams of the Great Smokies.

Muddy water can be the companion of high water. As long as water conditions are not hazardous, continue to fish even if the water is off-color. Since a fisherman's biggest challenge on any day is sneaking up on trout, and because a trout has to believe the fly is real in order to eat it, muddy water completely masks your presence from the trout. It also obscures your fly well enough that it is extremely hard to discern from a natural. Water usually becomes muddy after a downpour of rain. This sudden surge in the stream not only picks up silt and sand, but nymphs and terrestrial insects as well. Trout, particularly older and wiser ones, are aware of this and will usually occupy prime feeding stations as the water rises and grows murky. They are comfortable feeding under these conditions knowing that they can move about without being detected by herons, king fishers, or other predators. Muddy water is not usually good for dry fly fishing. However, large nymphs and streamers are completely in their element.

Many people believe that fishermen who consistently catch large trout have a secret "go to" fly. The truth is that even large trout will eat a wide variety of flies, secret or otherwise. I have to admit that I have my own personal favorite flies for bigger trout. They are among the most popular trout flies in the Smokies: Prince Nymphs, Tellico Nymphs, and bead-head Pheasant Tails. The most important quality a trout fly should have is that it should inspire confidence in the fisherman, and if you are confident in your fly, you will spend far more time keeping it in the water, drifting it through productive runs, and less time changing flies and tying knots. Many fishermen believe that a large trout can only be caught on a large sculpin streamer tied with half a rabbit skin tied on a size 2/0 hook. But basic everyday flies will usually outfish them. Smoky Mountain streams are not that fertile and large trout did not get that way by passing up easy meals. Nymphs, and even dry flies drifted into the path of a good brown, will often get eaten.

I remember one mild, drizzly December morning when I was fishing with Jack Gregory, my mentor when it comes to brown trout. The warm rain brought the cold stream to life, and as we made our way up the stream, Jack pointed out a large brown holding a few feet away from the bank upstream of our position. The trout was in a run of water less than two feet deep. Jack skillfully cast a size 12 Bead-head Pheasant Tail just upstream of the fish. The nymph had barely started its drift when the brown surged at the fly. The fight was on! After a few exciting moments in the rapids I helped Jack land the brown. It measured 22-inches long—a true Southern Appalachian trophy. Later, when we recounted the tale, Jack was asked what fly the brown ate. After hearing it was a Pheasant Tail Nymph one fisherman said, "Aw come on! What did you really catch it on?" Most people have a hard time believing that the same fly they're fishing can have results so much better than theirs. After Jack released that huge brown, I remember that he expressed some regret that he hadn't thrown a Thunderhead or Royal Wulff at him. The greedy take showed that the trout wasn't about to let anything get past him, and this was a clear example to me that the fly was not the element that made the catch. Jack had actually spooked that trout the day before and knew where to look for it. That morning he made an approach that wouldn't betray his presence and made a perfect cast before the fish knew what was going on.

Most big trout are spotted when they're running away from us. This is an unfortunate incident that has a

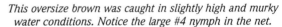

This oversize brown was caught in slightly high and murky water conditions. Notice the large #4 nymph in the net.

silver lining. You now know where this trout spends some of its time. Chances are, the next time you come to the stream under similar conditions, he will be there. If at all possible, come back in a few hours, or even the next day. The longer you wait, the more conditions will change, possibly forcing that fish to move. Then again, that spot may always host a nice trout, so commit the location to memory. You may need to write down the spot, as well as the conditions, in a fishing journal but I usually tend to replay the event in my mind so many times that it becomes indelibly etched there.

Another way to find big browns is to simply go looking for them. A good pair of polarized sunglasses is needed, and remember that looking for a good one will require far more walking and looking than actual fishing. The best time to look for a big one is when fish are really hitting. If most of the trout in the creek are eating, you can bet the big ones are feeding as well. After all, they didn't get big by not eating. You will need to exercise some restraint though, because if you have to fish for every small trout you find, you will never get around to spotting a big one. Any good vantage point where you can see into a pool is a good place to start. You may be surprised how many fish you spook while doing this. It is not unusual to see ten or more trout of all sizes darting up a pool as you peep down on them. The biggest fish will see the smaller scattering trout, or even sucker fish, as a signal to move to their hiding spots so it is imperative that you keep as low a profile as possible. Definitely dress in earth-tone clothing so you won't stick out against the background. More importantly, try not to view from a point where you will be silhouetted against the sky. This will make you stick out regardless of what you're wearing. Also, be careful not to cast shadows on the water.

One of the most important things you can do to help your chances of hooking a good fish is to keep wading to a minimum. One evening, several of my best fishing buddies came over for dinner and we eventually pulled out photo albums to relive some glory days. I was struck by the fact that we were not wearing wading gear in over half of the shots where we were holding big trout. Many of the remaining photos with waders were made possible when the trout were hooked after a cast was made from the bank. Just as you are accutely aware of a car pulling into your driveway late at night, a large trout will be on guard when he hears someone wading the creek. Big fish get that way by being overly cautious.

Intentionally fishing for larger trout in the Smokies requires a different state of mind than merely going out to wet a line. If you just want to catch trout and enjoy the day, your chances to hook a large trout are usually less than if you have a plan to look for big trout. If you are targeting larger browns, you will probably have a very slow day as far as catching fish goes. Large browns are relatively few and far between. No one hooks up every time they try. Large streamers used to lure big browns are not very effective on

Looking down from above with polarized sunglasses is an extremely effective way of spotting good fish.

the average Smoky Mountain rainbow and may even spook smaller trout. These smaller trout often attempt to eat the larger nymphs you cast, but hook-ups are few since they may not grab they fly by the hook. Fishing a size 8 or 10 nymph is a good way to catch greater numbers of fish while still having a shot at a good one.

If you happen to find a good fish feeding, chances are good that others are also active. Cloudy, rainy days are the best, but I have experienced enough "average" days on the stream when it seemed big trout were feeding in all the right places. If you happen to spook or miss a good fish in a likely spot, chances are good that other big fish will be active in other prime feeding lanes. Target likely lies and runs where you have seen a big trout, or drift nymphs and streamers under every rock you can find. While this is the best strategy, big browns still have a habit of being unpredictable.

If you happen to find a good fish, don't call the taxidermist just yet. Finding a large brown and hooking him are two different things. In fact, if you do hook a large

Can you find the big brown? This fish is well over 20" long. This fish actually wedged himself out of sight under this rock after the photo was taken.

Smoky Mountain brown, chances are the two of you will part company before he's brought to hand. First of all, notice how the trout is behaving. If he's glued to the bottom in deep, slow water there is a minimal chance he will cooperate. If he is in a shallow riffle and frequently moving about in order to feed, chances are good he will eat. Unless your trout is rising or exceptionally high in the water, a dry fly should be ruled out. Large trout get big by making every calorie count. Rising can use more energy than eating drifting nymphs or emergers. Big browns stationed in shallow riffles, or the head of runs, will often eat small nymphs as well as large ones. Use the largest hook size you believe you can get away with because this is not a big river environment where there is plenty of open water for a trout to run and wear down. Remember that a large fish in the Smoky Mountains has a multitude of snags and will use these to his advantage. A small hook will not hold the bony jaw of a large fish as well as a large hook when he's running down rapids and boring under boulders.

Large hooks are not possible in all instances, though. If a large fly will spook the fish, or if only small flies are hatching, you may need to consider a small fly just to have a chance to hook-up. Tim Doyle, a skilled Smoky Mountain fly fishing guide once hooked and landed a brown over 24-inches long on a size 16 Bead-Head Pheasant Tail Nymph. He chose that fly because there was a good hatch of Blue Quill mayflies which are actually about the same size. A

fishing buddy of his had caught a fleeting glimpse of the feeding trout. The huge brown would not move far to feed on such small insects so the drift had to be precise. Taking it slow and easy was difficult on Tim's harried nerves. On what was probably about the thirtieth cast, the leader and line flinched and Tim hung into the big brown. Once the trophy was hooked, Tim was barely halfway there. Before Tim could even catch his breath, the brown was leaving the pool and running down the creek, taking him on a physical and emotional roller coaster ride through rapids and stream side snags. Tim had the fly on 4X tippet which eventually helped him beach the fish some 100 yards downstream. The most important thing that contributed to Tim's catch was that he was in the right place at the right time. Secondly, the fly was presented to the brown without alerting him to any impending danger. Also, there was a good degree of persistence that should be factored in. Once the big brown was spotted, the fly was consistently presented in a slow and deliberate fashion until it was finally eaten.

Large browns feeding at the head of large pools will often hold deep where they can stay out of the swiftest currents yet they'll still be able to intercept most food. Figuring the velocity of the water, as well as the depth, usually adds up to a very heavy rig. Large stonefly patterns often do well in this situation, but be sure your fly has enough weight to get down to the fish because trout in these type of feeding lanes seldom move much. They are usually positioned so every good morsel flows right to them. A good drift, with enough weight to drop through the current, will often draw a strike, but be patient. Getting a fly to fall through upwelling currents and drift to your fish is easier said than done. The perfect drift may come on your first shot or your sixty-eighth cast. Be careful the whole time not to spook the trout or give away your presence.

This brown was finally landed after following it well over 100 yards downstream. The 3X tippet I used was frayed and ready to give out after the fight. Photo by Tim Doyle.

Big browns will definitely eat big flies. Notice this brown's mouth compared to mine. I probably weigh 25 times more than the fish but his mouth is bigger. Photo by Tim Doyle.

Don't be shy about using large flies and if you hope to land a big trout you will need suitable tippet. Many tailwater trout fishermen are accustomed to using small flies with 6X or 7X tippet. When I tell them that I often prefer large nymphs, they assume I mean a size 12. My favorite Tellico Nymph for average to high water conditions is a size 6 with rubber legs, tail, and antennae. Dry fly purists and tailwater midge fishermen sometimes recoil in dismay, but keep in mind, that the larger size allows for plenty of weight to help it sink and it is pretty accurate when it's compared to the size of a natural stonefly nymph. Many eastern fishermen aren't used to fishing with western-size flies, but nevertheless, heavy tippet is required to turn over flies of this size. I usually use 3X or 2X for large nymphs and streamers. While this is strong tippet, I have been broken off enough times to make me consider stronger tippet if only it wasn't so thick and stiff. Swift currents, boulders, and snags give large trout plenty of opportunity to break your tippet.

Streamers work well as attractors when fished blindly to likely places. Big browns that are hidden from you are usually less aware of you. Slowly drifting a streamer, while twitching or hopping it, will draw startling strikes. Streamers can be fished at any time but seem to produce best in average to high water conditions. Streamers are also a favorite when streams are muddy or off-color. Patterns that have a lot of action seem to work best. For example, the up-and-down motion of a Clouser Minnow entices plenty of strikes. One fly that has become a favorite over the past few seasons is the Double Bunny. The action of the rabbit hair is very lifelike. Then again, tried and true Woolly Buggers and Muddler Minnows should never be counted out. Large rubber-leg nymphs such as Girdle Bugs, Bitch Creeks, and Yuk Bugs can also do well dead drifted or twitched as a streamer. Trout may take them for salamanders which are more abundant in the Great Smokies than anywhere else.

Regardless of the fly or method you choose, you have to be in a good location. I guarantee you will be very lucky to catch a trout approaching 12 inches in streams like Walker Camp Prong or Forge Creek. The reason is because there are no brown trout in either of these streams. The best brown trout streams will be where you will have the most likely opportunity to hook a good one. Little River and Deep Creek are probably the best-known streams in the park with large browns, but Cataloochee Creek should not be overlooked though. A good population of browns, combined with spectacular habitat, make this a great stream for brown trout fishing. The Oconaluftee is a fine stream with plenty of browns in excess of 12 inches and Bradley Fork has been known to produce a good one on occasion. Straight Fork is among the least known of accessible quality brown trout streams. The Middle Prong of Little River does not seem to have a huge brown trout population but it always seems to keep a few large ones in unexpected places. All of the streams flowing into Fontana have good numbers of browns. Hazel Creek would most likely be voted the top brown trout stream of the bunch, but Forney and Noland creeks are sleepers. Since there is less pressure on these streams, good fish are probably a little less wary.

This Deep Creek brown trout clobbered a Double Bunny streamer.

Trout Flies for the Great Smoky Mountains

A wide variety of fly patterns will catch trout in the Great Smoky Mountains, but some seem to have proven track records that help them to show up in fly boxes year after year. This list of common trout flies contains patterns often used in the Smokies. Many of the nymphs listed are often fished as a bead head. Fly patterns that are commonly used in Southern Appalachian streams, but not well-known outside of the region are listed separately.

Dry Flies
Adams, sizes 10-20
Elk Hair Caddis, sizes 14-18
Parachute Adams, sizes 12-20
Light Cahill, sizes 14-18
Quill Gordon, sizes 10-14
March Brown, sizes 10-14
Hendrickson, size 14
Blue Dun, sizes 10-16
Blue Quill, sizes 16-20
Stimulators, sizes 10-18
Blue Wing Olive, sizes 16-20
Comparaduns, sizes 14-18
Sparkle Duns, sizes 14-18
Bivisible, sizes 14-16
Royal Wulff, sizes 10-18
Royal Coachman, sizes 12-16
Royal Trude, sizes 12-16
Irresistible, sizes 12-16

Nymphs
Pheasant Tail Nymph, sizes 12-18
Hare's Ear Nymph, sizes 12-18
Prince Nymph, sizes 8-16
Kauffman Stonefly Nymphs, sizes 6-10
Soft Hackles, sizes 14-16
Bitch Creek, sizes 6-10
Zug Bug, sizes 12-16
Montana Stone, sizes 8-12

Streamers
Woolly Buggers, sizes 4-10
Muddler Minnow, sizes 4-10
Clouser Minnow, sizes 6-10
Double Bunny, sizes 4-6
Spruce Fly, sizes 6-10
Gray Ghost, sizes 6-10
Zonkers sizes, 4-10

Smoky Mountain Trout Flies
The Southern Appalachians have a fly fishing heritage that is largely unknown outside of the Southeast. Nowhere is the heritage more evident than in the fly patterns developed on these streams.

❧ Crow Fly ❧
This fly's ugly appearance does little to reveal its stellar performance. A close relative of the legendary Yellarhammer, trout must take this pattern for a large stonefly nymph.
Hook: Standard streamer hook, sizes 6-10.
Thread: Black 6/0.
Underbody: Lead wire or substitute.
Hackle: Split biot quill from a crow or starling, which will split and wrap best after soaking in warm water.
Body: Black yarn, floss, or peacock herl.

❧ George Nymph ❧
Developed in the 1930s for use on the Little River by the late Eddie George, the George Nymph is one of the most versatile patterns to come out of the Smokies. This pattern works well in a variety of situations, and it has even enjoyed success on Tennessee tailwaters where the trout are notoriously finicky eaters.

Hook: Standard nymph hook.
Thread: Black 6/0.
Underbody: Lead wire or substitute only on back half of hook.
Tail: Brown hackle tied in at a downward angle at bend of hook.
Back: Turkey tail or quill only covering abdomen.
Abdomen: Peacock herl
Wing Case: White poly yarn or Antron.
Thorax: Brown wet fly hackle, 2 or 3 wraps.

❧ Hazel Creek ❧
Once widely used in the Smokies, the Hazel Creek is an excellent summertime attractor, and it is also a good imitation of Light Cahill or Sulphur mayflies. While it seems to be losing its appeal with twenty-first century fly fishers, it is as appealing as ever to Smoky Mountain trout.
Hook: Standard dry fly hook, sizes 12-16.
Thread: Yellow or cream 6/0.
Wings: Cream hackle tips.

Smoky Mt. Park Fly Plate
by Ian Rutter

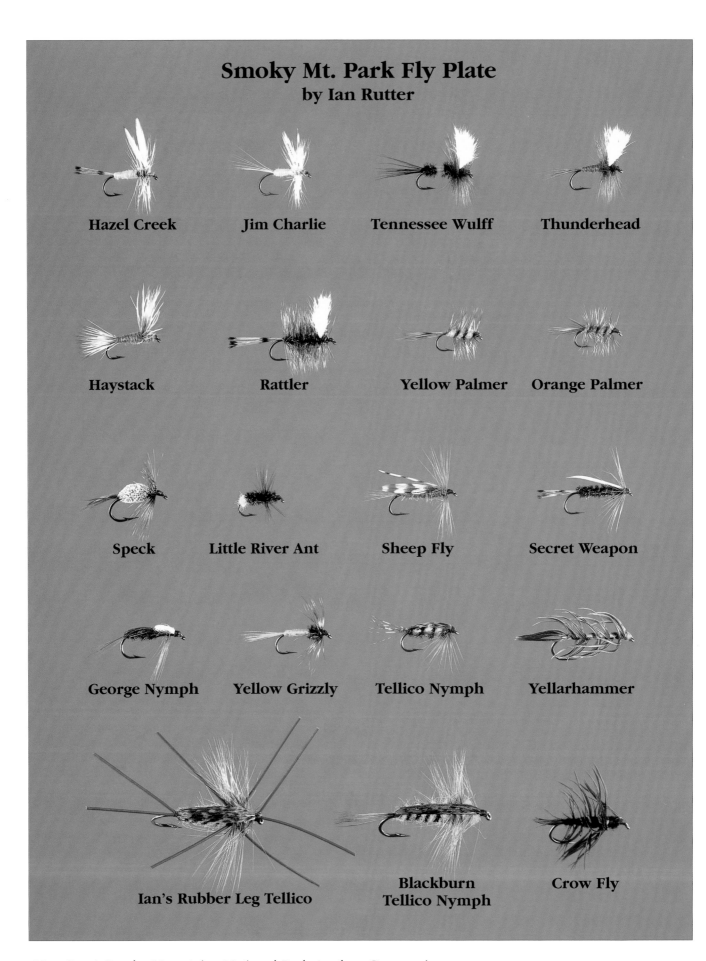

Hazel Creek

Jim Charlie

Tennessee Wulff

Thunderhead

Haystack

Rattler

Yellow Palmer

Orange Palmer

Speck

Little River Ant

Sheep Fly

Secret Weapon

George Nymph

Yellow Grizzly

Tellico Nymph

Yellarhammer

Ian's Rubber Leg Tellico

Blackburn
Tellico Nymph

Crow Fly

Tail: Golden pheasant tippets.
Body: Yellow dry fly dubbing.
Hackle: Grizzley and brown or ginger dry fly hackle.

❧ Haystack ❧

The Haystack is the ancestor of today's Comparadun and Sparkle Dun patterns. Relatively easy and inexpensive to tie, the Haystack is an excellent rough-water hatch matcher. The buoyant hair floats well and can withstand plenty of abuse.

Hook: Standard dry fly hook, sizes 12-16.
Thread: Black or gray 6/0.
Wings: Elk or deer hair.
Tail: Elk or deer hair.
Body: Gray dry fly dubbing.

❧ Jim Charlie ❧

This western North Carolina favorite is most effective when fished during the summer months. It is also an acceptable imitation of a Light Cahill, and will fool trout that are probably watching for Little Yellow Stoneflies.

Hook: Standard dry fly hook, sizes 10-16.
Thread: Yellow 6/0.
Wings: Grizzly hen.
Tail: Ginger and grizzly hackle fibers.
Body: Yellow dry fly dubbing.
Hackle: Ginger and grizzly dry fly hackle.

❧ Little River Ant ❧

This terrestrial pattern is a wet fly that is tied backwards. The fly is supposed to represent an ant carrying an egg.

Hook: Standard nymph or wet fly, sizes 12-18.
Thread: Black 6/0.
Egg: Pale yellow dubbing.
Body: Peacock herl.
Hackle: Black wet fly hackle tied in center of fly.

❧ Palmer: Yellow and Orange ❧

Palmers are among the easiest dry fly patterns to tie. Tied in either yellow or orange, they are exceptionally effective. The yellow palmer can look like an imitation of the Little Yellow Stonefly that is so common during late spring and into the summer.

Hook: Dry fly hook, 1X long, sizes 10-14.
Thread: Black 6/0.
Tail: Grizzly and brown hackle fibers.
Hackle: Palmered grizzly and brown dry fly hackle.
Body: Yellow or orange dry fly dubbing.

❧ Rattler ❧

If you need an attractor that will float well and remain visible, you may have found your fly. This pattern is most effective when fished in rough waters, or in streams with uneducated trout. In order to float the fly lower in the water, some fishermen clip the hackle off of the bottom of the fly.

Hook: Dry fly hook, 1X long, sizes 10-14.
Thread: Black 6/0.
Wing: Calf body or tail.
Tail: Golden pheasant tippets.
Hackle: Brown and grizzly wrapped the full length of the hook.

❧ Secret Weapon ❧

The Secret Weapon is the Smoky Mountain version of the Prince Nymph, but the main difference is that this fly has a tail of golden pheasant tippets.

Hook: Nymph hook, 1X long, sizes 10-14.
Underbody: Lead wire or substitute.
Thread: Black 6/0.
Tail: Golden pheasant tippets.
Rib: Copper wire.
Body: Peacock herl.
Wings: White goose biots.
Hackle: Brown wet fly hackle.

❧ Sheep Fly ❧

Most commonly fished on the Davidson River in North Carolina, the Sheep Fly is highly effective in park waters. Popularized by the Howell family of fly fishermen in Brevard, this pattern has been the downfall of many large trout in the mountains of western North Carolina.

Hook: Nymph hook, 1X long.
Thread: Black 6/0.
Tail: Brown hackle fibers.
Body: Muskrat or Adams gray dubbing.
Wings: Grizzly hackles tied in shiny side up.
Hackle: Brown wet fly hackle.

❧ Speck ❧

Possibly the most unusual and least recognized Southern Appalachian fly pattern, the Speck is devastating. In spite of its clipped hair body, the Speck is a wet fly. Originally developed on the Tellico River, this pattern mirrored the Adams Irrestible dry fly but was adapted to the wet fly techniques favored by fishermen in the area. While we may never know for sure, it is probably safe to assume that trout mistake the fly for a cased caddis larva.

Hook: Standard nymph hook.
Thread: Black 6/0.
Tail: Brown hackle.
Body: 2 or 3 small clumps of caribou hair spun and clipped to shape.
Hackle: Brown and grizzly wet fly hackle.

❧ Tellico Nymph ❧

One of the most important Southern Appalachian patterns, the Tellico Nymph is effective all-year long. This fly was named for the Tellico River in the mountains south of the Smokies where it was developed. It is meant to imitate common Golden and Little Yellow stoneflies. The Blackburn Tellico, developed by Richard Blackburn, is more popular among fishermen that prefer large Tellico Nymphs, but I have also listed my own rubber-leg version of it as well. This variation has proven effective on even the most jaded brown trout.

Hook: Nymph hook, 1X long, sizes 8-16.
Underbody: Lead wire or substitute covered with yellow yarn to smooth over uneven edges.
Thread: Brown, black, or pale yellow 6/0.
Tail: Guinea hackle fibers.
Back: Turkey tail or quill.
Rib: Peacock herl.
Body: Yellow floss.
Hackle: Brown Chinese rooster hackle collar or beard style.

Blackburn Tellico Nymph

Hook: Standard streamer hook, or 3X long nymph hook, sizes 6-10.
Underbody: Lead wire or substitute covered with yellow yarn to smooth over uneven edges.
Thread: Brown, black, or pale yellow 6/0.
Tail: Mink guard hair.
Back: Turkey tail or quill.
Rib: Peacock herl.
Body: Golden Stone color nymph dubbing.
Hackle: Brown Chinese rooster neck hackle palmered.

Ian's Rubber Leg Tellico Nymph

Hook: Standard streamer hook, or 3X long nymph hook, sizes 6-10.
Underbody: Lead wire or substitute covered with yellow yarn to smooth over uneven edges.
Thread: Brown, black, or pale yellow 6/0.
Tail: Brown rubber.
Back: Turkey tail or quill.
Rib: Peacock herl.
Body: Golden Stone color nymph dubbing.
Legs: Brown rubber.
Hackle: Brown Chinese rooster neck hackle palmered.
Antenna: Brown rubber.

Tennessee Wulff

The Tennessee Wulff is a variation of the universally known Royal Wulff, with the only substitution being that of the chartreuse floss instead of the characteristic red.
Hook: Standard dry fly sizes, 10-16.
Thread: Black 6/0.
Wings: Calf body or tail.
Tail: Brown hackle fibers, moose body hair, or elk mane.
Body: Peacock herl and chartreuse floss.
Hackle: Brown or coachman-brown dry fly hackle.

Thunderhead

The Thunderhead is the king of Smoky Mountain attractor dry flies. This heavily hackled Wulff-style fly floats well, and is highly visible in the pocket water that is so common in these streams. The Thunderhead seems to have lost some of its potency on the most heavily fished streams, but it is still a killer in the back country.
Hook: Standard dry fly hook, sizes 10-18.
Thread: Black 6/0.
Wing: Calf body or calf tail.
Tail: Brown hackle fibers.
Body: Adams gray dubbing or muskrat.
Hackle: Brown rooster neck or saddle hackle.

Yellarhammer

Without a doubt, the Yellarhammer is the most legendary of Smoky Mountain trout flies. Before the days of efficient interstate commerce, Smoky Mountain fly tyers had to make due with what they had. The feathers of the Yellow Flicker made for excellent trout catchers and the Yellarhammer took its title from the name locals called the yellow woodpecker. It is now illegal to kill Yellow Flickers or sell their feathers. However, dove or quail biot quills, dyed yellow, are extremely hard to distinguish from the real thing. Grizzly hen, dyed yellow, is also used with success on smaller hook sizes. There are nearly as many variations on the Yellarhammer as there are tyers tying them. Following are the two most common incarnations.

Hook: Standard streamer hook, sizes 4-10.
Optional Underbody: Lead wire or substitute covered with yellow yarn to smooth edges.
Thread: Yellow 6/0.
Hackle: Split primary wing feather from dove or quail dyed golden yellow. Splits and wraps best when soaked for at least ten minutes.
Body: Yellow floss.

Hook: Standard nymph hook, sizes 8-12.
Thread: Yellow or black 6/0.
Tail: Grizzly dyed yellow hackle fibers.
Abdomen: Yellow floss.
Thorax: Peacock herl.
Hackle: Grizzly hen dyed yellow.

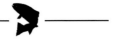

Part II: Stream Descriptions
Bryson City, North Carolina

Bryson City is one of the most charming small towns a trout fisherman could ever visit. Situated on the banks of the Tuckaseegee River, Bryson City has managed to maintain a quiet, unassuming atmosphere, and after a few hours in town, you may expect to see characters from the Andy Griffith Show strolling the sidewalks. Large hotels are rare, but both country inns and bed and breakfasts are available and restaurants are not in short supply either. There are more than enough eateries to satisfy anyone on a typical stay of several days to a week.

Deep Creek is the principal fishery, with Noland Creek a noteworthy second. But the Tuckaseegee is not a trout stream; this large river is home to smallmouth bass, walleye, and the like, through Bryson City. The Nantahala is also worth noting. Since it is not within the boundaries of the national park, this tailwater stream—with quality trout fishing—is only a short drive from town. Whitewater paddling is more popular than trout fishing on the Nantahala so show up early or late to dodge the constant parade of kayaks and rafts. Streams in the Cherokee area are only a short drive from Bryson City. Fontana Lake is not far either. However, unless you bring your own boat you should not expect to be able to make a day trip to Hazel or Eagle creeks. Forney Creek is accessible by taking the trail from the end of Lakeview Drive but should only be considered a day trip for fit hikers.

Swain County Chamber
of Commerce
PO Box 509-W
Bryson City, NC 28713
800-867-9246
www.greatsmokies.com

Bryson City is a small town with great trout fishing in every direction.

Bear Creek

Bear Creek is a small tributary of Forney Creek that was restored with native brook trout by the National Park service in 2005. Rainbows and browns are still present in lower pools near the confluence with Forney Creek. Campsite #75 is on Bear Ceeek, but it is far better to stay at campsite #74 on Forney Creek because it is only a short distance from Bear Creek. This stream should be viewed as a side trip on an extended stay at Forney Creek rather than as a destination in itself.

Deep Creek

Deep Creek is among the most heralded streams in the Great Smoky Mountains because it has been known for its trout fishing since the early days when sportsmen first began making trips to the southern highlands. Deep Creek is the only stream in the park where brown trout are the predominate species. Rainbows often account for the bulk of the catch, though, since browns are extremely wary. The two types of fish extend all the way up the Deep Creek watershed, only giving way when the stream gets so small that only brookies can tolerate it. Fishermen are common close to the campground, but there are less as you travel into the back country.

Most of the fishing pressure on the creek takes place in the lower two miles that are found between the park line and the Deep Creek Loop Trail intersection. The area in the campground and just upstream are the most popular in the fall, winter, and spring, but this one-mile stretch of creek will be inundated with inner tubers from Memorial Day until Labor Day. Therefore, summer fishing

Bryson City Area

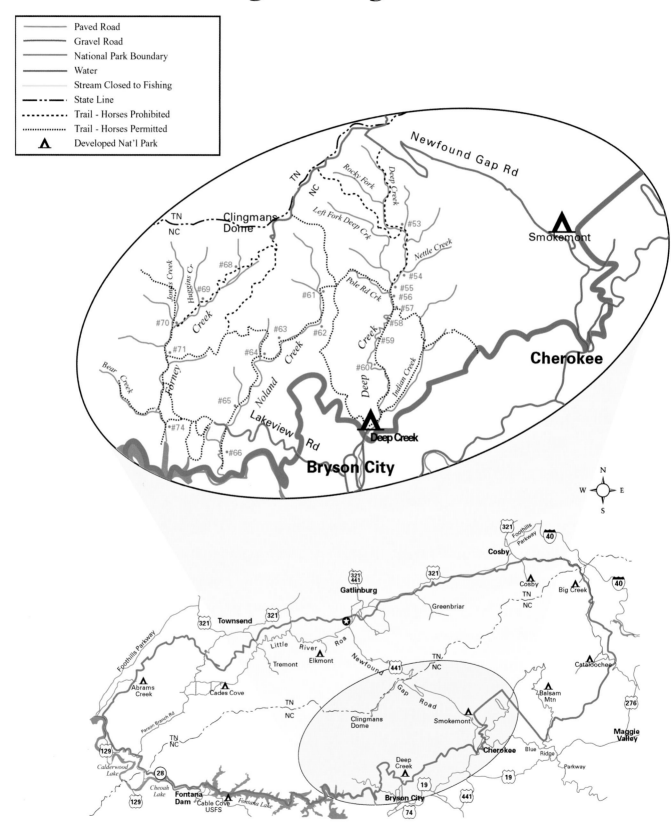

Deep Creek is among the best brown trout streams in the Great Smoky Mountains

is only practical very early or late in the season. Remember, though, that fish in this section are often less skittish due to their acclimation to tubers. (Tubing is prohibited upstream of Indian Creek, about one mile from the campground.)

Once you reach Campsite #60, access becomes spotty for several miles. The trail takes a lot of ups and downs and has most of its access near the back-country campsites. Fishing pressure is extremely light in this section but you should take a buddy when fishing any part of this section because if you are injured, it could be a while before you were found. The area between Campsites #60 and #57 could take several days to fish so don't strike out on a mission to cover that distance in a day.

Access regains some consistency once the trail reaches Campsite #57—known as The Bryson Place. Horace Kephart had his last permanent camp here before he died. He wrote about the mountain people, their customs, as well as sporting topics. He was a major proponent for the formation of a national park in the Smokies. This campsite is the most popular one on the creek and can accommodate up to 20 campers and a dozen horses.

An alternate route into Deep Creek is to take the Deep Creek Trail from Newfound Gap Road down to the stream. It is a two-mile walk down the mountain before you reach the stream, and the virgin forest probably looks the same as when Horace Kephart walked the creek. Most fishermen taking this route walk as far as Campsite #53, then begin fishing their way back. Rainbows and browns are evenly distributed in this stretch. As you make your way upstream, you should pick up a few brookies. Most fishermen catch at least one when making this trip.

The walk back out is a tough uphill climb, but enough fishermen have done it before you to know it can be done. As tough as it is, many proclaim that they have made two trips into upper Deep Creek in one day: their first and last.

Forney Creek

Forney Creek is among the most remote of the large streams in the Great Smokies, and during my many years of fishing and hiking in the Smokies, I have only found a handful of fishermen who have visited this Fontana Lake tributary. Cataloochee is often referred to as a forgotten corner of the park, with Forney Creek being so neglected that few have ever even known of its existence in order to forget about it.

There are no roads to take you to this stream, only trails or the useage of a boat, can get you there. Shuttles from Fontana Marina are tougher to negotiate than Eagle or Hazel creeks because Forney Creek is much further away. If you have your own boat, the best place to launch would be at the Swain County Park on the Nantahala arm of Fontana Lake near Almond, North Carolina.

Forney Creek

The walk-in angler will do best to start at the tunnel at the end of Lakeview Drive, sometimes better known as the Road to Nowhere. Use a map since there are several trail intersections along the way, few of which give directions to Forney Creek. The 3.6-mile walk is relatively mild, and will take between an hour-and-a-half to two hours to reach the creek near back-country Campsite #74. The few fishermen encountered will probably be on horseback or under the burden of a backpack. The hike in and out prohibits all but the most physically fit and fanatical from making this a day trip.

The long stretches of pocket water, broken by the occasional big pool, make this ideal water for fishing bushy dry fly patterns. Rainbows are generally eager and can be found throughout the watershed. But the browns, while more secretive and less prevalent, are often less cautious here than in more pressured streams. They are present all along the stream, even well upstream of Jonas Creek. Look for them in eddies and feeding lanes that flow near cover, with the largest specimens surely being found in the largest pools in the creek.

The Forney Creek Trail follows the stream along its entire course, but probably only provides about 50 percent access along the best water downstream of Jonas Creek.

Be careful to watch the trail markers. Keeping an eye more to the water than the trail will guarantee that you will stray from the trail as others have before you. If the path becomes faint, or you find several logs placed across the trail in a row, turn around and you will probably find the real trail.

Those arriving by boat will prefer Campsite #74 as it is close to the lake. Those moving upstream to Campsites #71 or #70 have more water to choose from, but #71 is also a popular horse camp. While the privacy will be plentiful at Campsites #69 and #68, the stream will be much smaller and the fishing will not be as productive. By the time the stream reaches Campsite #68, it is fairly small and is extremely steep with cascades and waterfalls being the norm. This also makes fishing these waters rather hazardous. While prime fishing is not a requirement for a back-country trip, I must admit that if I'm putting in a good deal of effort, I want the best water possible. In my experience, fishing below the confluence with Huggins Creek has been far better than the fishing upstream of there.

Huggins Creek

Huggins Creek is a remote tributary of Forney Creek. Located far out—in the upper reaches of the watershed—this is one of the more difficult streams to visit. An overnight stay at Campsite #69 is the best way to make the trip. Huggins Creek is primarily a rainbow trout stream but the odd brown may turn up, and brook trout begin to show as you go further upstream. (These are the last brookies in the Forney Creek watershed.)

Huggins Creek is currently closed to fishing about a mile upstream of its confluence with Forney Creek in order to protect this remnant population. Use caution if you do venture up this stream since no trail follows it. This could be an awful spot to turn an ankle.

Indian Creek

Indian Creek is Deep Creek's first major tributary upstream of the Deep Creek Campground. Indian Creek does not recieve much fishing pressure, and is probably best known to fishermen as the point where tubing is prohibited on Deep Creek. Only about one mile from the campground, Indian Creek should be kept in mind. If Deep Creek is too crowded, or if the water is too high, Indian Creek may save the day.

Most of this stream is under dense cover but there are enough places to drop a fly that make it worth the trouble. General attractor patterns are all that is needed to fool these trout.

Jonas Creek

Jonas Creek is a major tributary of Forney Creek and one of the most out of the way streams in the Smokies. This small stream has spots with tight casting conditions, but the trout are gullible. Campsite #70 is situated at the confluence of Jonas and Forney creeks. If you camp here, you should stay several days in order to properly dedicate time to fishing both forks, taking advantage of the privacy afforded by such a remote location.

Left Fork of Deep Creek

Deep Creek's left fork is among the least accessible of the streams in the Smokies. The largest tributary of Deep

Indian Creek Falls

Creek, its confluence is well masked and there is no trail that follows it. While it is smaller than the mainstream of Deep Creek, its quality of fishing is not less. Browns are common, as well as rainbows, and brookies are present here, but it is doubtful that many fishermen ever find themselves far enough upstream to catch any.

The best way to fish the Left Fork of Deep Creek is to camp at Campsite #55. Several days should be allowed so that you can properly explore Deep Creek as well. The Left Fork confluence is just upstream of the campsite. Reservations are recommended for this site since it is popular with horseback riders.

Nettle Creek

Nettle Creek is a small tributary of Deep Creek that enters the stream near Campsite #54. Nettle Creek should only be chosen over Deep Creek if you have already packed in and high water is an issue.

Noland Creek

Noland Creek is easy to find and is usually a peaceful place to spend a day trout fishing because its neighbor, Deep Creek, gets far more fishing pressure. Noland Creek flows into the Tuckaseegee arm of Fontana Lake. While boat access is possible, it is impractical since it is much easier to just drive to the creek.

The Noland Creek Trailhead is about one-mile upstream of the lake. The trail is not well marked from the road, yet is can be found along the left side of a large parking area, just before the road crosses a bridge. If you make it all the way to the tunnel, you have gone too far.

Rainbows are the most common catch in Noland Creek but browns have established a firm foothold in this watershed and are present in all areas that are accessible. Noland Creek is a small watershed and only has a few tributaries. For this reason, it does not seem to get much smaller as you travel upstream.

The trail is an old road and very easy for hikers. Is used to lead to Salola Valley, which was once a thriving community on Noland Creek, but that was before the construction of Fontana Dam and the formation of the park.

A possible overnight route into Noland Creek is via the Noland Divide Trail which starts on Clingmans Dome Road. The trail in is all downhill though, so you may want to arrange to have a car waiting for you on Lakeview Drive at an appointed time. Because it's a punitive walk back up Noland Divide, nearly to the top of Clingmans Dome, save your energy for fishing.

Pole Road Creek

This Deep Creek tributary is only of minor interest. A considerable walk—past much of the quality water of Deep Creek—is required to reach this small stream. Therefore, this destination is best thought of as a sidebar on a longer trip.

Campsite #55 is situated just across Deep Creek from Pole Road Creek. This is a fairly popular campsite so reservations are recommended.

Rocky Fork

Rocky Fork is one of the headwater tributaries of Deep Creek. A rigorous walk up Deep Creek, or down Deep Creek Trail from Highway 441, is required. Rainbows and browns are common, but brookies are probably too far upstream and this will prevent any realistic fishing opportunity for most fishermen.

Since it is only a small stream, Rocky Fork should lose out in a choice between it and Deep Creek.

Larger pools like this one will often hold the largest trout in Noland Creek

Cherokee, North Carolina

The Qualla Reservation at Cherokee, North Carolina borders the southern edge of the national park. Cherokee has a number of hotels, campgrounds and restaurants as well as a casino for anyone who wishes to try their luck. Fishermen will find themselves at home here. The Oconaluftee River, Raven Fork, and Soco Creek all flow through the reservation and are heavily stocked with rainbows, browns, and brookies.

A daily permit is required to fish on the reservation, but the tribal permit is not valid inside the national park. North Carolina fishing licenses are not available on the reservation, so you may want to pick one up on the way.

The Oconaluftee River, Straight Fork, and Bradley Fork are the principal park streams around Cherokee, and it is only a short drive from Cherokee to the streams around Bryson City. While it is a longer trip, Cataloochee Valley, near Maggie Valley, North Carolina, is also a possible day trip.

For information regarding
Cherokee, North Carolina:
800-438-1601
www.cherokee-nc.com

Local Fishing Information:
Smoky Mountain Fly Fishing
626 Tsali Blvd.
Cherokee, NC 28719
828-497-1555
www.smokymountainflyfishing.com

Beech Flats Prong

Beech Flats Prong is a headwater stream of the Oconaluftee River. It shadows Highway 441 but is relatively tough to approach because of steep slopes, dense vegetation, and a general lack of trails. Rainbows are predominant in the lower reaches, with brown trout that occasionally exceed 12 inches. But browns eventually disappear and brook trout take their place as the stream ascends the slopes and gets smaller under the dense forest canopy. At this point, brook trout become more common and rainbows dwindle as well. While this stream was never closed to fishing, it became legal to keep brook trout over seven inches here in 2002.

Bradley Fork

Bradley Fork flows through Smokemont Campground just before it joins the Oconaluftee River on its way to Cherokee and the Tuckaseegee River. Smokemont is the perfect place to base a trout fishing camp. Plenty of rainbows and browns can be caught right in the campground, and in fact, some of the prettiest water on the stream is in the campground.

Fishermen thin out as you hike upstream on the Bradley Fork Trail, and brook trout seem to slowly appear above Chasteen Creek with the the best opportunities to catch one being upstream of Taywa Creek. Taywa is currently closed to fishing. Browns are not as common as

Cherokee Area

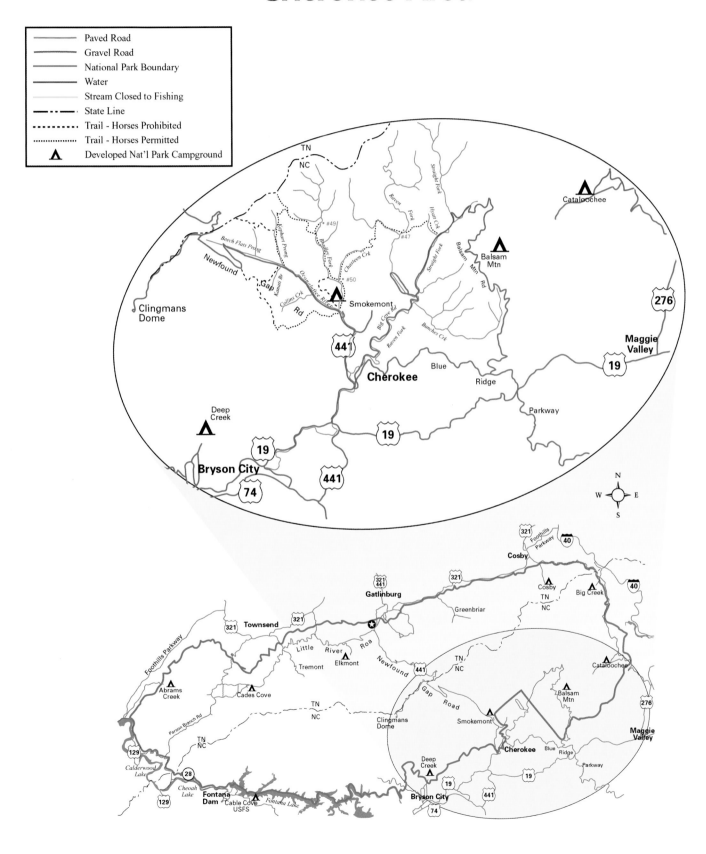

Legend

	Paved Road
	Gravel Road
	National Park Boundary
	Water
	Stream Closed to Fishing
	State Line
	Trail - Horses Prohibited
	Trail - Horses Permitted
⛺	Developed Nat'l Park Campground

TN
NC

Straight Fork

Cataloochee

Raven Fork

Hyatt Crk

Beech Flats Prong

Newfound

Kephart Prong

Balsam Mtn Rd

#49

Balsam Mtn

Bradley Fork

Chasteen Crk

Straight Fork

276

Gap

Kanati Br

#47

Collins Crk

#50

Oconaluftee River

Rd

Smokemont

Clingmans Dome

Big Cove Rd

Raven Fork

Bunches Crk

Maggie Valley

441

19

Blue

Cherokee

Ridge

Parkway

Deep Creek

19

Bryson City

441

74

N

W   E

S

321

Foothills Parkway

40

Cosby

321

Cosby

Big Creek

40

321
441

Gatlinburg

Greenbriar

TN
NC

Townsend

321

Little

River

Roa

Newfound

Cataloochee

321

Tremont

Elkmont

441

TN
NC

Balsam Mtn

Foothills Parkway

Abrams Creek

Cades Cove

TN
NC

Clingmans Dome

Gap   Road

276

Parson Branch Rd

Smokemont

Maggie Valley

TN
NC

129

Cherokee

Blue   Ridge

Calderwood Lake

28

Deep Creek

Parkway

Cheoah Lake

19

129

Fontana Dam

Cable Cove
USFS

Fontana Lake

19

Bryson City

74

441

rainbows, but are present all the way to the closed water at Chasm and Gulf Prongs.

Back-country camping is available at Campsites #49 and #50. (Campsite #50 is actually on Chasteen Creek but only a short distance from Bradley Fork.) Check with the back-country office before heading out, though. These campsites have a history of being closed due to bear activity.

Bunches Creek

Bunches Creek is the most difficult stream to access that is open for brook trout fishing but it may be the best. Opened to fishing in 2002, Bunches has decent numbers of legal sized brookies. The secluded nature of this stream should assure a solitary day of trout fishing.

Chasteen Creek

Chasteen is the most noteworthy tributary of Bradley Fork. It is only about a mile up the easy Bradley Fork Trail from Smokemont so it is worth checking out if you're camping there for several days. Campsite #50 is an easy place for the backpacker to pack in to and set up camp.

This stream is small and casting conditions are tight so bring a short rod. However, the trout are greedy enough to usually reward the cast that makes it to the water. Browns have been a pleasant surprise for me in this stream. I usually catch at least one 10- to 12-inch brown which always seems a bit too big for this small stream.

Collins Creek

Collins Creek is a small tributary that is worth exploring but only for the small stream fanatic because casting conditions on this stream will test any seasoned small stream fisherman. It flows through a small picnic area before joining its flow with that of the Oconaluftee.

This stream is your best bet to get a grand slam on the Oconaluftee. After catching a rainbow and brown on the 'Luftee, a short trip up Collins can provide the elusive spec. You may even be able to get a slam by only fishing Collins Creek. Though usually small, rainbows and browns are present, but browns are least likely to be caught. However, a few surprisingly good-sized browns have come from the lower end of this unlikely looking stream.

Hyatt Creek

Hyatt Creek is only a small tributary of Straight Fork and is easy to overlook. Only small stream fanatics need to consider this one. Rainbows and a few browns are near the

junction with Straight Fork, but the stream quickly turns to brookies after this point.

Access is not easy even though Hyatt Ridge Trail stays nearby. Rhododendrons keep the creek well hidden.

Once, while hiking this trail into Raven Fork I noticed something wriggling in a shallow ford across Hyatt Creek. I quickly snatched up what I assumed would be a salamander. To my surprise I had caught a 4-inch brook trout barehanded.

Kanati Branch

Kanati Branch is a small brook trout stream that enters from the west side of Highway 441. This stream can be tough to spot, so keep your eyes open for the stream on the west side of the highway, just north of the Kephart Prong Trail. The Kenati Branch Trail doesn't provide much access to the stream.

This is a small stream with tight conditions. In fact, that may be an understatement. Come armed with your best bow and arrow cast.

Kephart Prong

Kephart Prong is a lightly fished stream composed almost entirely of rainbow trout. Browns have also colonized this stream but are a relatively rare catch. Access can be found off of the Kephart Prong Trail which follows the stream as far as the Kephart shelter.

Oconaluftee River

The Oconaluftee River has one of the most melodic names of any stream in the Smokies. Flowing from the slopes of Mount Kephart, Beech Flats Prong and Kephart Prong join to become the Oconaluftee River. When flowing through the national park, the stream is of moderate size throughout most of its flow. But the waters of the Raven Fork eventually join it, doubling the size of the river just before it leaves the park and meanders through the Qualla reservation at Cherokee, North Carolina.

The 'Luftee doesn't seem to receive the pressure that it should considering the access afforded by Highway 441. There are far fewer pull offs than other roadside streams like the Little River and the West Prong of the Little Pigeon. However, there are enough to find a place to fish. One reason for the lack of crowded fishing conditions may be where the Oconaluftee is geographically situated. Fishermen from Tennessee must drive the full length of the West Prong of the Little Pigeon. Many will also have to pass up Little River, while others may have to cross the Middle Prong of the Little Pigeon. North Carolina anglers must deny the temptations of some of their most heralded streams—like the Nantahala and Tuckaseegee rivers, and Deep, Noland, and Cataloochee creeks. Still others are waylaid by the heavily-stocked streams in Cherokee. There is no way to reach the Oconaluftee without passing up quality trout water.

Those who decide to pass up other streams for the Oconaluftee will not be disappointed. Like most streams in the park, rainbows account for the bulk of the game fish. However, browns are exceedingly common.

The Oconaluftee runs a fairly straight course so it is mostly composed of pockets and runs, with most of the large pools located downstream of the Smokemont Campground because it is there where the Bradley Fork flows in and the 'Luftee becomes a larger stream. But the lack of large pools above this point may be a blessing in disguise for the fishermen. I have hooked, or spooked, more good trout from unlikely spots on the 'Luftee than on any other Smoky Mountain stream.

The apparent lack of pressure and abundant broken water may explain why good fish come readily to bushy attractor patterns. Be alert and look for good lies that provide cover, as well as a good flow of water. On the lower end, the large meadows that border the river also make terrestrial fishing productive during the summer and early fall.

Raven Fork

The raven plays a central role in Cherokee mythology. When the world was created, Raven flew over it all. When he grew tired, his wings dipped to the earth and created the Smokies. The Raven Fork is at the center of the Cherokee culture in western North Carolina and flows from virgin forests of hemlock, poplar, maple and spruce.

This is without a doubt the largest stream with brook trout in the Great Smoky Mountains National Park. Unfortunately, the rugged nature of the terrain affords only a minimum of access. A day trip is possible, but prepare for a grueling hike.

The most practical route for a day trip is to park on Straight Fork Road and hike in via the Hyatt Rige Trail. It is about two miles of hiking uphill and one mile down to the stream. The Enloe Creek Trail crosses Raven Fork on a large steel bridge just upstream of Enloe Creek. Campsite #47 is just across the bridge and is a great place to stay for the night. (This campsite also accomodates horses.)

This is not a stream to consider when water conditions are even moderately high or when flash flooding is a possibility. The massive size of the stream bed, when compared to the size of the water, assures me that this stream can hold some water. Considering the fact that the stream must be negotiated without getting on the rhododendron choked banks, I also recommend that this trip be made when water conditions are on the low side. Don't forget too that Raven Fork's high elevation keeps water temperatures cool even during the hottest part of the summer.

Raven Fork is very rough downstream of the bridge and I have never cared to negotiate it. There are no trails along the stream to make the trip an easy one, and the banks are steep and thick with vegetation. Waterfalls in this gorge only make the difficult trip more dangerous. Going upstream is a better choice. However, remember that every step you take will be retraced in the stream bed.

Rainbows and brookies seem to share the stream well. The absence of logging in this watershed probably spared these brookies the same fate as those in other parts of the Smokies. Due to the relatively large size of the stream, there is reason to hope for a nine- or ten-inch brook trout, although most will be under seven inches.

Far downstream of here, the Raven Fork flows along Big Cove Road in Cherokee and is stocked intensively with rainbow, brown, and brook trout. Upstream of its junction with Straight Fork, from there until the park line, the stream is reserved for members of the Eastern Band of Cherokee. And the area near the park line is on private property, making it inaccessible. There are also no trails that follow the creek upstream.

Straight Fork

Straight Fork is an excellent trout stream that receives little attention from most fishermen. The stream is very accessible thanks to Straight Fork Road, a gravel road that follows it for about five miles inside the park. Straight Fork flows about a mile outside of the park to its confluence with Raven Fork and the intersection with Big Cove Road. This mile of water though, outside of the park, is reserved for members of the Eastern Band of Cherokee. You will pass a tribal trout hatchery just before entering the park.

The roadside portion of the stream is rainbow and brown trout chowder. Every pocket has a trout, sometimes even two, but once the road fords the stream there is no easy access. Your only choice is to wade up the stream. From this point, browns seem to become less common and brookies begin to show up. The further you go, the better your chances will be to hook a brook trout.

Fontana Lake, North Carolina

Standing 480-feet tall, Fontana Dam is the highest dam in the eastern United States. The massive dam was originally built during World War II to provide power for Oak Ridge, Tennessee and the Manhattan Project. The atomic bombs dropped on Japan were the end result. The Little Tennessee River once flowed where Fontana stands.

Streams in this section of the park are the least crowded. The relative difficulty of access accounts for this—not the quality of fishing. The fishing is excellent, and if you figure in the solitude and seclusion, you get some of the best wild freestone trout streams in the Southeast.

Fontana Dam is closest to the Bryson City area, but it is still almost an hour away. The drive from the Townsend and Cades Cove area is not far but it's time consuming. Over Deals Gap, the twists and turns of Highway 129 are unbelievable. One 11-mile section of the road between Chilhowee Lake and the state line has 316 curves. You may be able to see your own headlights in your rear view mirror. Use caution if you drive this stretch of highway. It is extremely popular with motorcyclists who spend the day zipping back and forth through the curves.

Accomodations in the area are few. Fontana Village is the principle place to stay if you are planning a visit that does not include camping. There are no developed campgrounds in the park, but there is a nice Forest Service campground and boat ramp at Cable Cove. Bring anything you need with you because there is only a small store at Fontana Village.

Most of the fishing in this section of the park is on the other side of Fontana Lake. A ferry is available from Fontana Marina to both Eagle and Hazel creeks. If you bring your own boat you can launch from either Fontana Marina or Cable Cove. Rental boats and canoes are available at the marina.

Most of the streams in this chapter require crossing Fontana Lake by ferry or with your own boat.

Fontana Village
PO Box 68 Highway 28 N
Fontana Dam, NC 28733
800-849-2258
www.fontanavillage.com

Local Fishing Information
and Ferry
Fontana Marina
800-849-2258 ext. 277

Bone Valley

Bone Valley Creek has what may be the most colorful name of any stream in the Smokies. Cattle were a fixture here in the days before the creation of the park. A late season blizzard killed most of the cattle herded into the valley one April during the 1870s. Their bleached bones littered the valley for years.

This stream can have some tight casting conditions since the undergrowth is thick due to the fact that the forest continues to recover. Rainbows are eager and usually small, and the population of brown trout allows for pleasant surprises. Brookies are somewhat less common, but catching one can become possible if you move into sections of the creek upstream of the end of the trail. Campsite #83, at the confluence of Bone Valley and Hazel creeks, is the ideal spot to spend some time while you explore this stream. Fishermen are not as thick here as they are on Hazel Creek and any fisherman spending time here owes it to himself to explore this beautiful piece of water.

Eagle Creek

Although no tougher for the boater to reach than Hazel Creek, Eagle Creek is overshadowed by its neighboring watershed. Eagle Creek is far easier to reach on foot than

Fontana Area

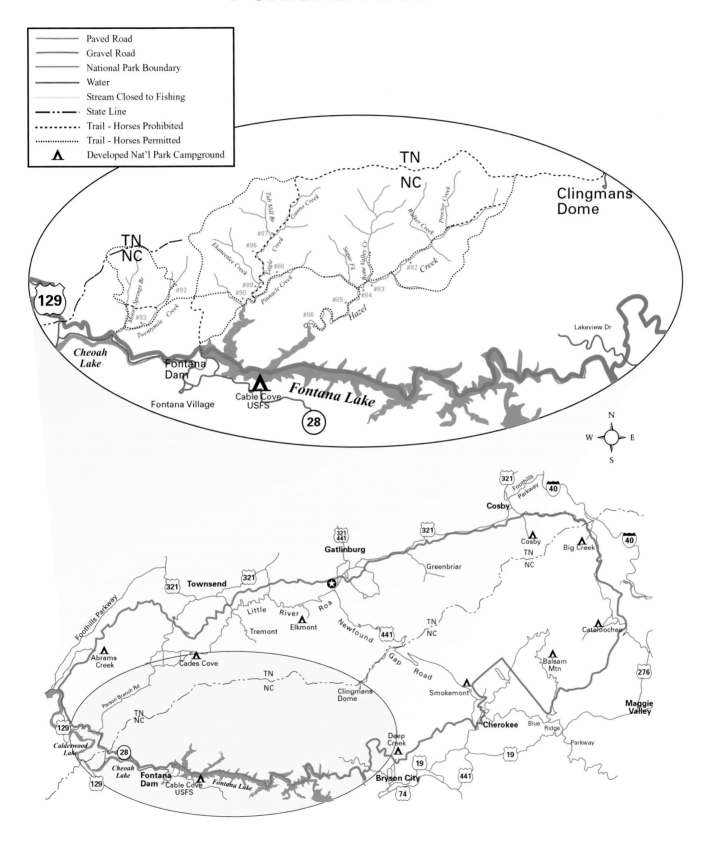

Legend:
- Paved Road
- Gravel Road
- National Park Boundary
- Water
- Stream Closed to Fishing
- State Line
- Trail - Horses Prohibited
- Trail - Horses Permitted
- ⛺ Developed Nat'l Park Campground

Clingmans Dome

TN / NC

Tub Mill Br Gunna Creek #97 #96 Eagle Creek Walker Creek Proctor Creek

TN / NC

#92 #88 Bone Valley Cr #82 Creek

Moore Springs Br #93 #89 #90 Pinnacle Creek Sugar Fk #85 #84 #83

Twentymile Creek #86 Hazel Lakeview Dr

Cheoah Lake

Fontana Dam

Cable Cove USFS Fontana Lake

Fontana Village

129 28

N / W / E / S

321 Foothills Parkway 40

Cosby

321 Cosby Big Creek 40

321 441 Gatlinburg TN / NC

Townsend 321 Greenbriar

Little River Road Newfound 441 TN / NC Cataloochee

Tremont Elkmont

Foothills Parkway Gap Road Balsam Mtn 276

Abrams Creek Cades Cove TN / NC Clingmans Dome Smokemont Maggie Valley

Parson Branch Rd TN / NC Cherokee Blue Ridge

129 Deep Creek 19 Parkway

Calderwood Lake 28 19

Cheoah Lake Fontana Dam Cable Cove USFS Fontana Lake Bryson City 441

129 74

Eagle Creek is among the least fished streams in the park.

results. While there is always the outside chance of hooking a nice brown, this stream should be visited more for its seclusion and beauty than trophy fishing opportunities.

Ekaneetlee Creek

Situated at the confluence of Ekaneetlee and Eagle creeks, Campsite #89 is the perfect place to stay and explore. Backpacking is the only option; horses are not allowed here and it is much too far for a day trip. There is no trail that follows Ekaneetlee Creek, so you will have to return to camp via the stream bed.

The rainbows are generally small but eager. If you go far enough upstream, you may catch one of the native specs still found in this stream.

Hazel Creek

Hazel Creek is regarded by many as the quintessential Smoky Mountain trout stream. While trout fishing here differs little from other streams in the park, it has a definite atmosphere. In spite of its remote location, fishermen are a fixture on this stream. Trout fishing at Hazel Creek is a tradition and part of the heritage of many Southern Appalachian fishermen. I once fished Hazel Creek with Andy Sonner who made his first trip there when he was only two-years old.

Campouts here are some of the most elaborate you will find anywhere. The scent of grilled steak often wafts on the breeze after darkness falls on the creek. Many campers employ Hazel-Creek-carts to lug in an inordinate amount of provisions and equipment. These buggies with large wheels are ferried across Fontana Lake to the former town of Proctor on Hazel Creek. There is little to see of the town now, except for the old Calhoun house and the ruins of the lumber mill.

Proctor was the largest of several thriving communities situated on Hazel Creek before the national park and was first settled and farmed by pioneers. Ritter Lumber Company later came in and Proctor became a boom town that went bust after the watershed was logged out. Over 200 million board feet of lumber were removed from the valley, feeding a growing nation between 1910 and 1928. A small historical exhibit at the bridge near the Calhoun house shows the location of Proctor landmarks, streets, and prominent buildings.

Horace Kephart made his first home in the Smokies on Sugar Fork, a small Hazel Creek tributary. Kephart was a librarian that came to the Smokies seeking seclusion after his marriage failed. He made his home here at the "Back of Beyond" making a living writing articles on hunting, fishing, and woodsmanship for sporting magazines of

Hazel Creek, but it still requires a 5.4-mile hike from Fontana Dam. Therefore, an overnight trip is the only realistic option. Fontana Marina is the closest launch to Eagle Creek, but Cable Cove is only a little bit further for motorized craft. Canoes should opt for launching at the marina.

Campsite #90 is ideal for boaters and offers the chance to hook a nice smallmouth in the creek embayment. In addition to smallies, largemouth bass frequent this area in the summer and walleye are a springtime possibility. Rainbows quickly dominate the stream, but the best fishing starts around the confluence with Ekaneetlee Creek at Campsite #89. Other good campsites to consider are #96 and #97. Campsite #96 is unique in that you are camping on an island in the creek. The next campsite up, #97, is at the confluence of Tub Mill Creek. If you have the rare fortune to share either of these campsites with other fishermen, make friends because the two of you are a rare breed.

Rainbows are by far the most numerous species in Eagle Creek, but browns are found in many of the likely spots. The trout of Eagle Creek are unfamiliar with the concept of selectivity so any reliable pattern should have good the day. He later moved to Deep Creek when the lumber company began logging on Sugar Fork.

Unless you have your own boat to take across Fontana Lake, a shuttle will be necessary from Fontana Marina. These are easy to arrange, although they are more practical for an extended stay, than for a simple day trip. If you intend to take your own boat across the lake, the boat ramp at Cable Cove is closer to Hazel Creek than the Fontana Marina. This is not particularly important for motorized boats, but will make a huge difference if you are paddling a canoe. You can plan on about a one-hour paddle across the lake and up the embayment if you take a canoe from Cable Cove. You can feel secure leaving your watercraft at the mouth of Hazel Creek as it is often done with instances of theft practically unheard of.

Trout fishing on the creek is good at the mouth but only gets better as you progress upstream. Smallmouth may be occasionally caught in the first mile, or so, and are extremely common in the creek embayment. In fact, largemouth bass cruise the embayment as well as walleye, white

The Hazel Creek pushcart can turn a backpack trip into a cushy camping trip complete with big breakfasts.

Hazel Creek is among the most legendary of Smoky Mountain streams. Its beauty and isolation make it a favorite with many fishermen

bass, and sunfish. Fishing will be very consistent from Campsite #85 on up the creek. Campsite #83, at the confluence of Bone Valley Creek, is the most popular on the creek, a favorite of fishermen, backpackers, and horse riders alike. Rainbows are the most common catch and browns are present in good numbers. The size of this stream, combined with the good brown trout population, means that there are plenty of stories swapped over the campfire about the one that got away. The trail becomes rougher above Campsite #83, so use of Hazel-Creek-carts is not advisable to reach Campsite #82.

You will have to journey above Campsite #82 before brookies begin to turn up. This is an excellent campsite to use as a base in order to explore upper Hazel Creek, Proctor Creek, and Walker Creek. As you approach Hazel Creek Cascades, the opportunity to catch a grand slam gets better. It is not uncommon to catch a grand slam out of just one good run in this part of the stream. The waters upstream of Hazel Creek Cascades only have specs. It was closed to fishing in 1975 due to the moratorium on brook trout fishing but was reopened in 2002. Up to five brookies over seven inches may be kept upstream of Proctor Creek. This stretch of water will surely re-establish its status as a favorite spot for catching native specs.

Moore Springs Branch

This is the only major tributary of Twentymile Creek. On this rhododendron infested stream, fishermen are as rare here as a clear cast.

Pinnacle Creek

This small stream is the first tributary on Eagle Creek travelling upstream from Fontana Lake. Campsite #88 provides camping here, but it is not the best place to stay if you're on a serious fishing trip.

Rainbows will be the standard catch, but fishing in Eagle Creek will be easier and possibly more rewarding. Campsite #90 is not that far from the stream and more accessible by boat.

Proctor Creek

Proctor Creek is a headwater tributary of Hazel Creek. Rainbows and browns are most common on the downstream end of the creek, but brookies will be in the mix throughout the stream. There is no trail on Proctor Creek, but back-country camping is available about one mile down Hazel Creek at Campsite #82.

Sugar Fork

Sugar Fork is the first sizable tributary on Hazel Creek as you travel upstream from Fontana Lake, but it is a small stream that is generally overlooked by fishermen enamored with Hazel Creek. Campsite #84, at the confluence of Sugar Fork and Hazel Creek, is a nice place to spend a few days, but Sugar Fork is not far from Campsites #85 and #83.

While the small trout in this stream are fun to catch, you will probably enjoy Hazel Creek, or nearby Bone Valley Creek, more.

Tub Mill Branch

This small branch qualifies as one the toughest streams to access in the Smokies. Campsite #97 is the closest point to stay, but no trails follow the stream. While the fishing can be good, casting conditions are tight. You don't have to make the tough trip to Tub Mill to fish for small rainbows in tight casting conditions.

Twentymile Creek

This is the only major stream in this chapter that does not require a trip across Fontana Lake. Twentymile Creek is one of the least visited streams in the park that may be reached by car. While only a small portion may be fished near your car, good access is afforded by the Twentymile Trail.

Rainbows are essentially all you will catch. They are generally small yet exceptionally greedy. That's good since the tight conditions make casting difficult.

Stocked brookies and browns are occasionally caught in the lower pools, just above the confluence with Cheoah Lake. (The lake is stocked by North Carolina and is not within the park boundaries.) If you fish the creek downstream of Highway 129, or in the embayment, a North Carolina fishing license is required and you must fish under current North Carolina regulations. Even though the brookies you will find in Twentymile are stockers, they are protected by park regulations.

Walker Creek

Walker Creek is a small, rarely fished tributary of Hazel Creek. Rainbows and brookies are the most common catch, but browns are present in the lower sections. Walker Creek merges with Hazel Creek about a half-mile upstream of Campsite #82.

Gatlinburg, Tennessee

Gatlinburg is easily the busiest town bordering the park and may be the best place to stay for fishermen who need to entertain families. Gatlinburg has a tremendous number of hotels, restaurants, and rental cabins. Numerous shops will please anyone who wants to shop for souvenirs. Outlet malls and theme parks are only a short drive away in Pigeon Forge. Gatlinburg also boasts a number of popular attractions including a saltwater aquarium.

The West Prong of the Little Pigeon flows through town and is stocked. A daily permit is required to fish in Gatlinburg, in addition to all other applicable fishing licenses. This is urban fishing, however, and many fishermen are far more comfortable fishing the forested streams of the park rather than the hotel-lined waters in Gatlinburg. Many of these streams may be easily reached from the Townsend area as well.

Mount Leconte is at the center of this section. Many of these streams flow from its slopes.

Gatlinburg Visitor & Convention Center
234 Airport Rd.
Gatlinburg, TN 37738
800-343-1475
www.gatlinburg-tennessee.com

Local Fishing Information:
Smoky Mountain Angler
466 Brookside Village Way, Suite 8
Gatlinburg, TN 37738
800-436-8746
www.smokymountainangler.com

Alum Cave Creek

Alum Cave Creek can be found at the Alum Cave Trail which ascends Mount Leconte. This small stream has hit-or-miss fishing for brookies and rainbows. This stream is highly acidic, and in fact, it is so acidic at times that trout will migrate out of it. Park Service surveys indicate that this stream is probably too acidic for trout to spawn successfully. This is shown by the fact that only adult trout are found here.

Cannon Creek

This small stream is not very hard to locate but may not be worth the effort. To find Cannon Creek get in Porter's Creek at the first foot bridge that crosses it. Cannon Creek plunges over a series of falls on the right about fifty yards upstream. Casting conditions are tight to say the least.

Cosby Creek

Cosby Creek is about a thirty minute drive from Gatlinburg in the small mountain town of Cosby. This small community has sometimes been referred to as the "Moonshine Capital of the World". Cosby Creek is a small pleasant stream that flows through Cosby campground. This is an excellent spot to camp and catch native brookies. It is legal to keep up to five brookies over seven inches upstream of the Rock Creek confluence as of 2002. Any rainbows you find will probably be downstream of the campground. The occasional stocked fish from Cosby makes its way in the park. You may fish the stream from the road to the campground or from the Low Gap trail which is on the opposite side of the creek. The trail also follows the creek upstream of the campground.

False Gap Prong

This is a small stream that is difficult to locate. Fish this stream only if you're on a mission to cover the least fished small streams.

Gatlinburg Area

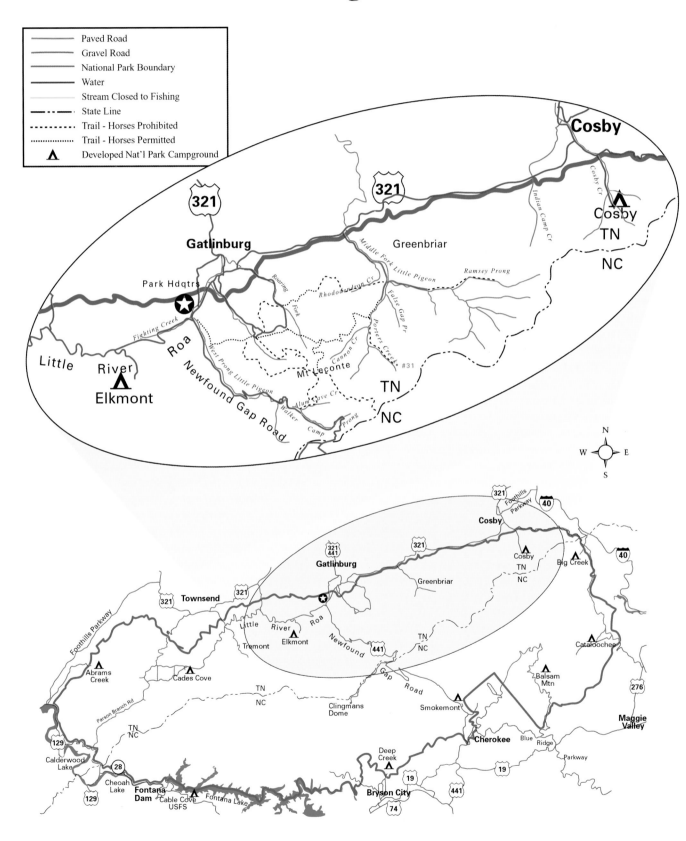

Fighting Creek

Fighting Creek can only be described as overlooked since it flows near one of the busiest intersections in the park yet it sees few, if any, fishermen. Entering the West Prong of the Little Pigeon at park headquarters, Fighting Creek parallels Little River Road briefly before flowing under the road and into obscurity. This small rainbow trout stream is never a top choice for fishermen but is valuable to remember in times of high water.

Indian Camp Creek

This is a rather small stream between Gatlinburg and Cosby but a good one for specs. It was closed in 1975 but reopened in 2002. Camping is available at Cosby Campground or commercial campgrounds along Highway 321. While this stream is not as large as nearby Cosby Creek, most small stream fishermen will enjoy exploring it. Trail access is only intermittent which

Greenbrier is a beautiful stream of deep pockets and plunge pools.

makes access tougher than Cosby Creek which has roadside and trail access.

Middle Prong Little Pigeon River

The Middle Prong of the Little Pigeon River is often referred to as Greenbriar by locals, and is a great place to take the family for a picnic, sneaking in some fishing for yourself.

Five miles of gravel road follow the stream from the park boundary to the Ramsey Cascades Trailhead. The lower mile below the ranger station is not worth fishing in the heat of summer. Decent smallmouth are sometimes caught in this stretch of water, though. Browns are present in the lower reaches of the stream but seem to be a rare catch.

The best water is upstream of the ranger station where rainbows are common in the big plunge pools. As you walk up the Ramsey Cascades Trail, brook trout begin to turn up. In fact, they seem to be the only game fish by the time Ramsey Prong enters the stream.

Above Ramsey Prong, there is no trail and the going can be very tough. Brookies swim under towering hemlocks and tulip poplars that have never been logged. Bring a buddy if your decide to fish this section of the stream. If you get hurt there is little chance that someone will find you.

About a mile-and-a-half above the last trail access, the Middle Prong splits into its headwater tributaries of Buck Fork, Chapman Prong, and Eagle Rocks Prong.

Porters Creek

This Greenbriar area stream is one of the most attractive you will ever see. The lower mile of the stream parallels the gravel road from its confluence with the Middle Prong of the Little Pigeon. From the trailhead access is spotty, mostly due to the elevation of the trail above the stream and the dense brush that must be penetrated. However, access is good enough that you should find your way to the water.

Traces of the community that stood here before the park are visible if you keep your eyes open. Stacked stone walls and steps appear at intervals along the trail.

After about a mile, the trail enters virgin forest and the huge hemlocks, poplars, and maples tower over the stream and trail. After you cross the first foot bridge over the stream, there is no point to walk the trail other than to take in the beauty of the forest.

Fishing is still good near this point, but seems to degrade significantly by the next point where access is manageable. Porters Creek flows off of the anakeesta-laden slopes of Mount Leconte. (Anakeesta is a rock formation that leeches acid-bearing iron pyrite into the water.) Trout have historically done well here, but the looming specter of acid rain seems to hit this stream hard. As the ph is already acidic, there is no margin for added acidity.

Ramsey Prong

Ramsey Prong can only be accessed via the Ramsey Cascades Trail which begins to follow the stream about a mile-and-a-half above the trailhead at its confluence with the Middle Prong of the Little Pigeon. Brookies are all you will catch. However, this stream does not seem to fish as well as it looks. The fishing declines as you go. The high acidity of the water makes the trout less abundant here than in other streams.

Rhododendron Creek

Considering its proximity to the Middle Prong of the Little Pigeon and Porter's Creek, there is little reason to fish this stream. You may want to search it out if the more open waters in the Greenbrier area don't challenge your casting skills. This is one creek that has truth in advertising.

Roaring Fork

Roaring Fork is a relatively small stream that can only be accessed by a short drive down the busy Gatlinburg strip. Turn onto Airport Road and follow all the signs for the Roaring Fork Loop.

While the trout are not unusually large, I have yet to meet a local fisherman that doesn't have fond memories of this stream. As the name suggests, plunge pools are the standard and the rainbows strike bushy dry flies with gusto. Automobile traffic is usually moderate but fishermen are rare, so the occasional big stocked rainbow from Gatlinburg will find its way into the lower sections of Roaring Fork.

As you exit the the loop you will find yourself back in Gatlinburg on Highway 321.

Walker Camp Prong

As Walker Camp Prong winds its way upstream, brook trout become a regular catch, although few achieve any size. Rainbows remain a possible catch as well.

The waters at this elevation are borderline for trout because of the acidic nature of the water. Walker Camp flows from the slopes of Anakeesta Ridge, from which, acid-bearing iron pyrite can easily disperse into the stream. Acid rain only exacerbates the problem. Soil can usually neutralize any acid in acid rain. However, since these soils are already saturated from their natural geology, acid rain may pose a serious threat if air pollution continues to increase

over the Smokies. In spite of the water chemistry, trout are still thriving. While this has long been a good stream to fish for brookies, it became legal to keep up to five them at least seven inches in length during the summer of 2002.

West Prong Little Pigeon River

The West Prong of the Little Pigeon flows off of the slopes of Anakeesta Ridge. The Chimney Tops, two rock spires, tower above the river opposite Mount Leconte. The West Prong of the Little Pigeon is a steep stream that seems to be one large plunge pool after another. Cabin-sized boulders separate the deep green pools. This stream tires out fishermen quicker than most. Fish a hole, and climb over a boulder. This is the order of the day. Rainbow trout are at home in the turbulent rapids and flourish in these cold waters, because the West Prong remains cold even during the dog days of summer. Downstream of the Sugarlands Visitor Center, large stocked rainbows from Gatlinburg are occasionally caught, as well as a rare smallmouth bass.

Highway 441, also known as Newfound Gap Road, follows the stream throughout its course, however, there are long stretches where it is not visible from the road. Quiet walkways are interspersed at regular intervals, though, and they all go to the stream. While you cannot see the river from these pull offs, you can usually hear the swift water flowing toward Gatlinburg. Most of these trails arrive at the water in only a few hundred yards and parallel the stream. This is a perfect opportunity to fish only minutes from your car and feel as though you're miles from civilization.

While walking this casual network of trails you may notice fences and cairns made of piled rocks. Although it is hard to believe, this mountainside was farmed by pioneers in the early days before the park. Known as the Sugarlands, it was a remote backwater that was often used as a hideout by outlaws and moonshiners. Horace Kephart's classic *Our Southern Highlanders* chronicles a manhunt on these slopes.

Brook trout begin to show up around the Chimneys Picnic Area and become more prevalent as you go upstream. The road veers away at the picnic area and stays high on the mountain slope above the river until it reaches the Chimney Tops Trailhead. Even though you may be in sight of the road while fishing this gorge, consider it to be a wilderness trip if you try it. The road is essentially inaccessible because of the steep slopes and dense vegetation. It is close to a two-mile trip up the river that is as steep as a horse's face.

The West Prong splits into its two headwater tributaries at the Chimney Tops Trailhead. The names of the streams may be a little confusing at this point. Walker Camp Prong follows the road to Newfound Gap. Road Prong follows the trail toward the Chimneys. Before the highway was in place, Road Prong followed the road that the Cherokee and pioneers followed over the mountains. Now Road Prong sees only hikers along its banks. Road Prong is closed to fishing at this writing.

The Chimneys tower above the West Prong of the Little Pigeon.

Maggie Valley / Waynesville, North Carolina

Of all the communities bordering the Great Smoky Mountains, Maggie Valley and Wayneville are the least convenient park streams. This should not deter a visit, however. If you or your companions have interests other than fishing in the park, these towns will suit you well. Golf, horseback riding, hiking, snow skiing and shopping are all available here. There are also streams outside of the park to try.

The streams described in this section are in the Big Creek and Cataloochee Creek watersheds. It should be understood that none of these streams are very close to any population centers. Maggie Valley is about 45 minutes from Cataloochee or Big Creek. Big Creek Campground is about 45 minutes from Gatlinburg. Cataloochee Valley is about 90 minutes from Cherokee or Gatlinburg.

Sunset over Cataloochee Valley.

Maggie Valley Visitors Center
www.maggievalley.com
www.waynesville.com

Local Fishing Information:
Lowe Guide Service
Waynesville, NC 28786
828-452-0039
www.loweguideservice.com

Big Creek

Big Creek is a steep Appalachian stream with rainbows that behave like small stream trout. This is a fairly large watershed with all of its headwater forks reaching well over 4,000 feet, and flash floods are common after heavy rains. Rarely crowded with fishermen, the large plunge pools and pockets are full of greedy fish, although few will be larger than eight inches.

The most fishing pressure is found in the campground. Above the campground though, you may have to put in a bit of walking. The trail is high above the creek on a steep slope. The stream bed is full of boulders and white water so you may reach an impassable spot that will force you to turn around.

After about a mile or so the stream rises to the level of the trail. Near this point you will come to the unmistakable Midnight Hole. This large plunge pool lies at the bottom of a six-foot drop. The water is so deep they say it's as dark as midnight. This is the point where many local fisherman begin a day of fishing, getting far ahead of anyone starting at the campground.

Only a short distance upstream of here, Mouse Creek drops over its namesake falls and joins Big Creek. Back-country camping is in the Walnut Bottoms area at Campsites #36 and #37 near the confluence of Swallow Fork. Check with the back-country office before setting out to camp here. These sites are often closed due to bear activity. Above this point, Big Creek splits into its many headwater forks, several of which are closed to fishing. The best opportunities to catch a brook trout are upstream of Walnut Bottoms.

Caldwell Fork

Caldwell Fork enters Cataloochee Creek across from the Cataloochee Campground. Small rainbows are common but browns are far from rare in the lowest stretches. Caldwell Fork Trail closely follows the stream and back-country camping is available at Campsite #41. The campsite is preferable to #41 because you will be able to fish several of the streams in Cataloochee Valley from this spot.

Maggie Valley Area

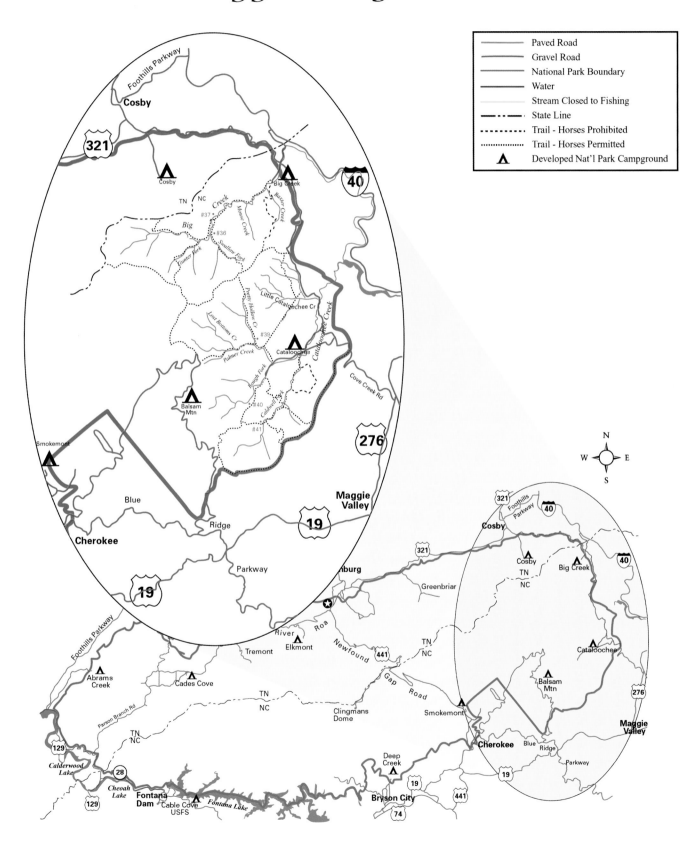

Legend:
- Paved Road
- Gravel Road
- National Park Boundary
- Water
- Stream Closed to Fishing
- State Line
- Trail - Horses Prohibited
- Trail - Horses Permitted
- Developed Nat'l Park Campground

Cosby

321

Foothills Parkway

TN / NC

Cosby

Big Creek

40

Big Creek

Mouse Creek

Baxter Creek

#37

#36

Swallow Fork

Gunter Fork

Pretty Hollow Cr.

Little Cataloochee Cr

Lost Bottoms Cr.

#38

Palmer Creek

Cataloochee

Cataloochee Creek

Cove Creek Rd

Balsam Mtn

Rough Fork

Caldwell Fork

#40

#41

276

Smokemont

Blue

Ridge

Maggie Valley

19

Cherokee

19

Parkway

N / S / E / W

321

Foothills Parkway

40

Cosby

Cosby

TN / NC

Big Creek

40

Cataloochee

Balsam Mtn

276

Smokemont

Maggie Valley

Cherokee

Blue Ridge

19

Parkway

Greenbriar

321

nburg

River Road

Tremont

Elkmont

Newfound

441

TN / NC

Gap Road

Clingmans Dome

TN / NC

Foothills Parkway

Abrams Creek

Cades Cove

TN / NC

Parson Branch Rd

TN / NC

129

Calderwood Lake

28

Cheoah Lake

Fontana Dam

Cable Cove USFS

Fontana Lake

129

Deep Creek

Bryson City

19

74

441

Smokemont

Cherokee

Cataloochee Creek

Cataloochee Creek holds a special place in the hearts of many fishermen. Tucked away in a secluded mountain valley, Cataloochee Creek is a world away and only Hazel Creek seems to excite fishermen as much. Cataloochee Creek is maintained by the park service to look the way it did in the middle of the 19th century. Homes of the Caldwell and Palmer families still stand, and there is also an effort under way to restore elk to this valley.

The last elk were hunted out of the Southern Appalachians by the middle 1850s. This area was chosen because of its excellent habitat and distance from civilized areas where they might do some damage. Elk are regularly sighted throughout the valley. Be sure to keep your distance as these are extremely powerful animals.

The best way to reach Cataloochee is via Cove Creek Road off of Exit 20 on I-40. From Maggie Valley take Highway 276 to I-40 and turn left on Cove Creek just before reaching the interstate. From this point, it is about a 10-mile drive. (There is a short stretch of gravel from the park line for about two miles.)

An alternate route is to take Exit 451 at Waterville. You will pass the Big Creek area. However, brace yourself for a 26-mile tooth rattler. The dirt road is a parade of potholes and washboards and requires a one-hour minimum of driving from the interstate. Although it is a longer route from Tennessee, the Maggie Valley Exit will be faster and more comfortable.

The ideal way to explore this scenic valley is to stay at Cataloochee Campground which is right on the creek. From here you can fish Cataloochee Creek and all of its tributaries. Arrive early since there are only 27 sites and they are first come, first serve. The campground is only open during spring, summer, and fall but the bathrooms are open all year. Check with park headquarters for specific opening and closing dates. Bring your groceries and

The meadows of Cataloochee Valley make for some of the best terrestrial fishing in the Smokies.

Calm water is abundant on Cataloochee Creek so use a stealthy approach.

fishing license since you will be almost an hour from a store.

Long riffles and pools separated by pocket water are what you will find. Some of the largest browns in the Smokies swim in Cataloochee Creek, but keep your expectations realistic. The typical catch will be rainbows and browns in the six- to ten-inch range. However, the competent fly caster can easily catch some foot-long trout during the best spring hatches. Much of the stream borders fields and pastures. This makes Cataloochee Creek one of the most productive streams to fish with terrestrial fly patterns.

Much of the water upstream of the campground is some distance from the road but not hard to reach. A short walk through the fields will get you there. The next time you see the creek next to the road will be where it splits into Palmer Creek and Rough Fork.

One of the prettiest pieces of dry fly water you might find anywhere is near Asbury Crossing. This is the third bridge over the creek downstream of the campground. Little Cataloochee Creek comes into the stream just downstream of here. The stretch of water from Asbury Crossing upstream to the next steel bridge is relatively hard to access. It is best to start at the lower bridge and fish your way upstream, but do not attempt this if the water is even moderately high. This is big water and can be hard to handle if the water is pushy. This should be considered an all-day excursion. (Access is even tougher downstream of Asbury Crossing with no trail or road crossings.)

Gunter Creek

This Big Creek tributary was opened in 2006. The stream is predominantly brook trout with a mix of rainbow trout as well. Don't expect to see another angler this far up the trail.

Little Cataloochee Creek

Little Cataloochee Creek is the least visible of the Cataloochee Creek tributaries. Located just down-stream of the Asbury Crossing bridge, you will have to wade your way up the stream to fish. There is no trail access. Correll Branch comes in on the right, about a mile up the creek. Most of the trout in Little Cataloochee will be five to eight inches long, but don't be surprised if you hook a brown over a foot in length.

Lost Bottoms Creek

Lost Bottoms is a tributary of Palmer Creek that was for-merly closed to fishing due to its strong population of brookies. Rainbows may also be caught near the conflu-ence with Palmer Creek. It is reasonable walk to make a day trip if you don't mind the hike. It is also a good stream to visit if you are on an extended camping trip at back-country site #39.

Mouse Creek

Mouse Creek is a tough stream to fish. It plunges over Mouse Creek Falls into Big Creek. But, there is no trail access on this small stream so if you decide to give it a try, you can expect to find small- to medium-size rainbows.

There is a waterfall about a mile-and-a-half upstream of the confluence with Big Creek. There are no fish above the falls.

Palmer Creek

Palmer Creek joins with Rough Fork to form Cataloochee Creek. A horse camp is located just upstream of the trail-head. This area was known as Indian Flats by Cataloochee residents before the park was formed. Rainbows are com-mon up and down the stream, but browns are only found in the lower sections. Brook trout start to appear upstream of Pretty Hollow Creek. Lost Bottoms Creek enters Palmer Creek about two-and-a-half miles upstream of the trail-head.

Pretty Hollow Creek

Pretty Hollow Creek is the biggest tributary of Palmer Creek. Pretty Hollow Gap Trail allows good access to the stream, and back-country Campsite #39 is a good base to

stay at if you want to fish Pretty Hollow as well as Palmer Creek. Check with the back-country office, though. Bears are often active in this area.

Rough Fork

Rough Fork flows past the old Caldwell homestead before joining Palmer Creek to form Cataloochee Creek. The lower section, before the confluence, is beautiful water bounded by fields and woods. Elk in the restoration effort are a common sight along this stream.

Casting is a little tougher once the stream leaves the meadows and is entirely in the forest. The Rough Fork Trail follows the creek for about a mile-and-a half to Campsite #40. Rainbows are comon up and down Rough Fork. Browns are most prevalent in the lowest reaches and brookies are most common upstream of #40.

Swallow Fork

Swallow Fork is a little fished headwater tributary of Big Creek, merging at an elevation of 3,000 feet. Access is available by following the Big Creek Trail from the camp-ground upstream to the Swallow Fork Trail. Most fisher-men are not able to deny Big Creek, so this leaves the trout in Swallow Fork rather uneducated.

A little over a mile upstream of the confluence of Big Creek and Swallow Fork, McGinty Creek enters the flow. Camping is available at Campsite #36, near the confluence of Big Creek and Swallow Fork.

Rough Fork flows through the old Caldwell homestead before joining Palmer Creek to form Cataloochee Creek.

Townsend, Tennessee

Townsend is the perfect retreat for fishermen seeking a quiet setting in which to fish. This small community is situated in Tuckaleechee Cove and borders the national park. Townsend has a number of hotels, rental cabins, and commercial campgrounds to stay in during your stay in the Smokies.

Nonfishing activities include hiking, tubing, swimming, and horseback riding. The shopping and attractions in Pigeon Forge and Gatlinburg are a little over 30-minutes away.

Little River flows through Townsend and its three prongs are only minutes from town. The scenic Cades Cove is also close by, including the fishing in Abrams Creek. Many of the streams in this section of the park are within easy reach of Gatlinburg.

Townsend lies in a valley adjacent to Cades Cove pictured here.

Smoky Mountain Visitors Bureau
7906 E. Lamer Alexander Parkway
Townsend, TN 37882
800-525-6834 • www.smokymountains.org
e-mail: smokymvb@chamber.blount.tn.us

Local Fishing Information:
Little River Outfitters
7807 E. Lamar Alexander Pkwy
Townsend, TN 37882
865-448-9459 • www.littleriveroutfitters.com

R&R Fly Fishing Smoky Mt. Guide Service
Ian & Charity Rutter
PO Box 60
Townsend, TN 37882
865-448-0467 • www.randrflyfishing.com

Abrams Creek

Abrams Creek has long been one of the most touted streams in the Great Smoky Mountains National Park—if not of all Southern Appalachia. Draining the scenic Cades Cove area of the park, Abrams is one of the most picturesque trout fishing destinations. Just making the drive through Cades Cove one can see upwards of 100 whitetail deer, a flock of wild turkeys, or perhaps a black bear perched high in a cherry tree eating his fill. Fishermen regularly report sightings of raccoons and river otters in the stream as well. The park service maintains this valley as it was when settlers first occupied it. Many cabins and a mill are maintained and open for visitation.

Cades Cove shows evidence of the antiquity of the Appalachian Mountains. Cades Cove and the Smokies were formed hundreds of millions of years ago when the continents of North America and Africa collided, an event known as the Appalachian Orogeny. A limestone plate was shoved from the depths of the earth to the surface. This limestone eroded at a faster rate than the surrounding geologic formations and became the valley that is Cades Cove.

This geologic phenomenon is also responsible for the conditions that make Abrams Creek notorious as a slick stream to wade. The fertile limestone waters allow for a variety of algae to grow on the bedrock bottom. Yet, long ago, when the limestone plate was shoved to the surface, it came up at an angle. This can be seen today by looking at the numerous sloped ledges that give Abrams Creek its signature look. The sloped bedrock bottom, combined with algae and silt, make for one of the slickest trout streams anywhere.

Abrams Creek is primarily a rainbow trout stream. There are some brown trout here, but they are much more rare than they used to be and there is no definitive explanation. The browns were covertly introduced to the Cades Cove section of Abrams Creek in the early 1970s and have flourished since then. In fact, several browns weighing five to ten pounds were caught over the years. Park service fisheries biologists shocked up a 7 ½-pound brown trout in 1994. Some believe that the massive flood of 1994 washed out most of the fish, but individual floods rarely extirpate trout populations.

Townsend Area

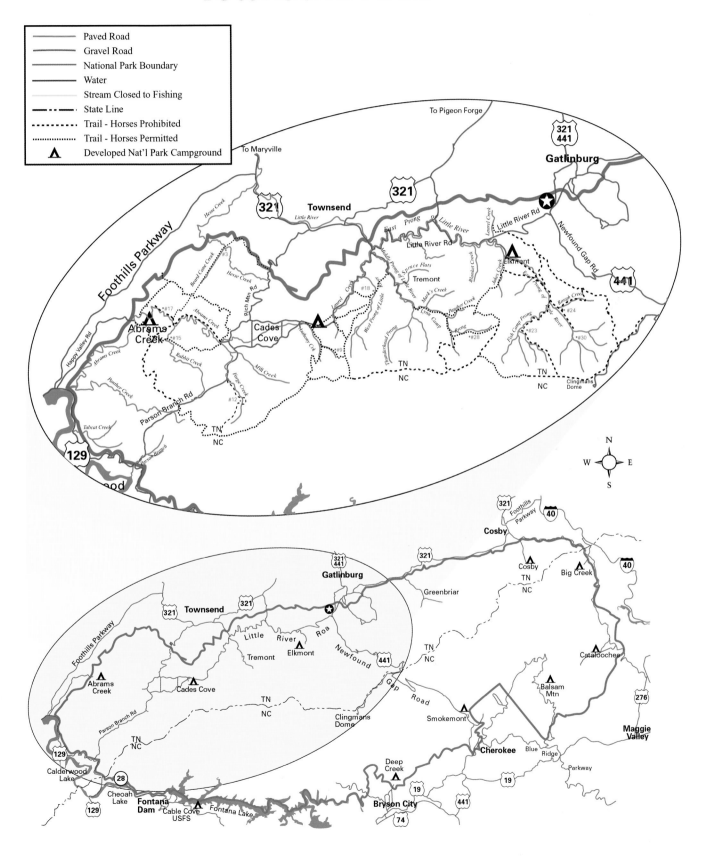

Legend:
- Paved Road
- Gravel Road
- National Park Boundary
- Water
- Stream Closed to Fishing
- State Line
- Trail - Horses Prohibited
- Trail - Horses Permitted
- Developed Nat'l Park Campground

To Pigeon Forge

321 441

Gatlinburg

321

To Maryville

321

Townsend

Little River

Foothills Parkway

Hesse Creek

Little River Rd

Little River Rd

Newfound Gap Rd

441

East Prong Of Little River

Laurel Creek

Bent Cane Creek

Hesse Creek

#3

Rich Mtn Rd

Spruce Flats

Blanket Creek

Ade Creek

Elkmont

#17

Abrams Creek

Abrams Creek

#15

#18

Laurel Creek

Middle Prong of Little River

Mark's Creek

Tremont

Panther Creek

East Prong of Little River

Rough Creek

#24

Happy Valley Rd

Rabbit Creek

Anthony CrA

#9

West Prong of Little

Thunderhead Prong

Lynn Camp

Prong

#28

Fish Camp Prong

#23

#30

Abrams Creek

Panther Creek

Parson Branch Rd

Mill Creek

TN
NC

TN
NC

Clingmans Dome

Tabcat Creek

Forge Creek

#12

TN
NC

Parson Branch

129

ood

N
W E
S

321

Foothills Parkway

40

Cosby

321

Cosby

TN
NC

Big Creek

40

321 441

Gatlinburg

Foothills Parkway

Townsend

321

Little   River   Roa

Newfound

Greenbriar

TN
NC

Tremont

Elkmont

441

Cataloochee

Abrams Creek

Cades Cove

Gap

Balsam Mtn

276

TN
NC

Road

Parson Branch Rd

TN
NC

Smokemont

Maggie Valley

129

TN
NC

Clingmans Dome

Cherokee

Blue

Ridge

Calderwood Lake

28

Deep Creek

19

Parkway

Cheoah Lake

Fontana Dam

Cable Cove
USFS

Fontana Lake

19

441

129

74

Bryson City

Trout in Abrams Creek seem to be a little bigger and are definitely stronger than fish of comparable size in other Smoky Mountain streams. The stream has an abundance of aquatic insects and snails that keep the fish well fed. However, like other park streams, don't expect to catch many over 12 inches. A 14-inch rainbow is a distinct possibility, but don't hold your breath.

There is no roadside access to Abrams Creek, but the stream can be fished from the trail that goes between the Abrams Falls Trailhead and the Abrams Creek Campground. This fact may lead some to believe that Abrams Creek offers only limited possibilities, but a look at a map will show several options.

Most of the fishing pressure is near the Abrams Falls Trailhead in Cades Cove. Upstream of the trailhead fishing can be exceptionally difficult but is a unique fishing experience in the park.

The bulk of Abrams's flow, through the center of Cades Cove, is in subterranean limestone formations. The water boils to the surface in numerous springs and the flow is almost completely restored to the surface by the time Abrams Creek flows under the loop road upstream of

Abrams Creek has a good number of rainbows over 12". Some are occasionally caught over 14" but these are rare.

the Abrams Creek parking area. Fishing in this spring creek section is best during slightly high water and even better if the water has some color. This area is productive with terrestrial insect imitations in the summer and fall.

The section of Abrams Creek that will yield the most stories from Smoky Mountain anglers is known as the horseshoe or the big shoe. Even a casual look at Abrams Creek on a map will reveal a large horseshoe bend that is nearly in the shape of a full, race-track oval.

A hiker that is unfamiliar with the area will probably notice that Abrams Creek winds away as he climbs Arbutus Ridge. It is a short climb and after descending the other side, about one-eigth of a mile, Abrams Creek rejoins the trail. However, if you decide to fish Abrams as it skirts Arbutus Ridge, count on a full two-mile jaunt through wilderness. There are no trails and leaving the stream will only place you in thickets of laurel and rhododendron. One Townsend old timer put it to me this way, "If a man plans to fish the big shoe he'd better bring his lunch and if things don't go well maybe his dinner and breakfast, too." At least a few fishermen spend an unplanned night in the horseshoe every year because they started too late in the day and darkness fell while they were still far from the trail.

A smaller horseshoe known as the baby shoe can be accessed directly above Abrams Falls. This is a smaller horseshoe but at least half a day should be set aside to fish this area because once again, the trail and stream are separated for about one mile.

Either of these horseshoes will probably guarantee a day of fishing in privacy. However, you should arrive early to be sure you get out before dark. This will also keep you from fishing behind another fishermen all day. If you fish these stretches of the creek you should plan to meet the wilderness on its own terms. A solo trip that results in injury or is stricken with foul weather will not be pleasant.

Stream access becomes more difficult downstream of Abrams Falls. The trail is often close to the creek but separated by thick brush and steep slopes much of the way.

Abrams Creek is a fertile stream thanks to limestone formations under Cades Cove.

This part of the stream receives little pressure and can make for a nice overnight trip.

There is a back-country campsite on the creek in the area known as Little Bottoms. Surprisingly few fishermen take advantage of this campsite and is about a two-mile hike from Abrams Creek Campground. July, August, and September are months for the trout fisherman to pass up the lower sections of Abrams Creek for other streams. Spring is another story, though.

The lower sections of Abrams Creek may be the best place in the park to hook a better than average rainbow. Little Bottoms does take some hiking to reach, and the large, still pools can be intimidating. However, fishing nymphs or caddis dry flies in the riffles can produce some surprises. The largest wild rainbow I've caught in the park was a 15 incher that ate an Elk Hair Caddis just upstream of Rabbit Creek, but I know several fishermen who have bested that.

There is some speculation as to whether or not these large rainbows are run-up fish from Chilhowee Lake. Chilhowee has a cold water discharge powerplant at the head of the lake that supports a year-round population of trout. Many believe that trout from Abrams Creek may lead dual lives, part of the time in the lake and part of the time in the stream.

Some claim that there is a steelhead run in the spring as the lake rainbows spawn. As much as I would like to exploit this angling gold mine, I have found that this is extremely hit or miss—mostly miss. Those trout that I have caught were nice, but not exactly worthy of the term steelhead.

Smallmouth and redeye bass become more common downstream of Little Bottoms. Many fishermen cast Royal Wulffs and Adams near Abrams Creek Campground only to find that creek shiners and chubs are the only fish interested. Very few fishermen employ the proper tactics because they are unaware that smallmouth and redeye bass are the predominant game fish. Muddler Minnows, Woolly Buggers, Clouser Minnows, and other streamers are usually the best flies to try for bass in Abrams. However, nymphs can also be effective. I've done well with rubber leg nymphs like bitch creeks, girdle bugs, and black rubber legs. Poppers work well, but are best in late spring and early summer.

From Little Bottoms to Chilhowee Lake is a long section of stream, perhaps 14 miles, that receives little to no fishing pressure. There are several reasons for this. Access is extremely difficult with the exception of the area near the Abrams Creek Campground. Taking a canoe or boat up the Abrams Creek arm of Chilhowee Lake is probably the best way to access the best bronze-backwaters in the park. Paddling in a canoe is also a great way to see a beaver or otter carrying on their daily routine. Proper caution should be used when fishing in this area. There are no trails along the creek. This section of Abrams Creek is one of the largest streams in the park, so wading can be hazardous in even mildly high water conditions.

Anthony Creek

Anthony Creek is the upstream flow of Abrams Creek, rising on the slopes of Bote Mountain below Spence Field. I'm not sure if anyone knows where Anthony Creek ends and Abrams Creek begins. Anthony Creek flows out of the Cades Cove Picnic Area into the open fields and pastures of the cove. As small branches join it, its size does not grow. Most of the water flows through subterranean limestone formations. The larger stream that emerges from springs, at the lower end of the cove, is Abrams Creek.

Generally small yet spunky rainbows are what the skilled angler will find. These trout are pretty eager and attack bushy dry flies with gusto. The trout in the picnic area are not as skittish as fish in other streams since they see throngs of harmless picnickers every day. This is an excellent piece of water to keep in mind if nearby Little River and Abrams Creek are too high to fish.

Upstream of the picnic area, the stream becomes a real challenge to fish. Negotiable pools are interspersed with long stretches of overgrown stream that demand creativity from a fly caster. Campsite #9 is an easy to reach place to pitch a tent on Anthony Creek.

Beard Cane Creek

Beard Cane Creek is a small stream that is difficult to access. Although not far from the park boundary in West Miller's Cove, there is no access from that direction. The only practical way is to hike in from Abrams Creek Campground or Cades Cove. Considering the small nature of the stream, its marginal elevation for trout, and the difficulty to access, you can easily find more productive destinations.

Blanket Creek

Blanket Creek is only worth mentioning for those fishermen who feel compelled to drop a fly in every trickle available. This small Little River tributary flows into the East Prong less than two miles downstream of the Elkmont intersection. It enters the stream on the opposite side from the road and is very easy to miss. It would be a good stream to fish when the water is too high if you did not have to cross the raging Little River to get there.

Fish Camp Prong

Approximately four-miles upstream from the Little River Trailhead, the river splits into two nearly equal forks—Little River to the left and Fish Camp Prong on the right. The stream confluence is only a short way up the Goshen Prong Trail just below a steel bridge.

Fish Camp Prong is definitely a noteworthy back-country fishing destination. Rainbow trout are caught most often, but browns are present in the lowest mile or so. However, Fish Camp Prong has an excellent population of brook trout in its upper reaches and fishing is very good. Its remote nature can assure you that most of these brookies see very few fishermen. Campsite #23 is a great place to stay and experience trout fishing as it was in the early days.

Forge Creek

This small stream is a tributary of Mill Creek in Cades Cove. Forge Creek is a paradox since you must negotiate the traffic of the Cades Cove Loop Road to reach the solitude this small stream offers.

Rainbows measuring five to eight inches are standard and casting room isn't that bad for such a small stream.

Forge Creek Road parallels and crosses the stream several times before reaching the Gregory Ridge Trailhead. Upstream, it runs along the Gregory Ridge Trail. The small rainbows in this section of stream see virtually no fishing pressure. This is a good stream to keep in mind if water conditions are high in larger streams.

Hesse Creek

Located in a tough spot, Hesse Creek requires a lengthy walk to reach. While you could probably expend equal or less effort for a better reward, Hesse Creek does have its points. Since it is in a part of the park with virtually no visitation, you will have the stream and Campsite #3 to yourself. (This campsite is at the confluence of Hesse and Beard Cane.) Unfortunately, once you reach Hesse Creek, there are no trails that follow it upstream or downstream. Beard Cane Creek does have a trail that follows it, but it is smaller than Hesse Creek.

Indian Flats Prong

Indian Flats Prong is a tributary of Lynn Camp Prong and it has all of its access via the Middle Prong Trail. It is about a two-and-a-half-mile hike from the trailhead.

Indian Flats is a mixture of brookies and rainbows, but is closed to fishing above the point where Middle Prong Trail crosses it.

Jakes Creek

Jakes Creek is an often overlooked stream. This is hard to believe since it actually merges with Little River in the bustle of Elkmont Campground. A productive couple of hours on Jakes Creek will turn up a good number of small rainbows and perhaps a few browns.

Trail access is sporadic and casting conditions will rate anywhere between negotiable, for the average caster, to difficult even for those accustomed to small streams. This is a good stream to keep in mind if water conditions are less than desirable on Little River.

Laurel Creek
(West Prong of Little River tributary)

Laurel Creek is the main tributary of West Prong of Little River and follows Laurel Creek Road that leads to Cades Cove. This small rainbow trout stream receives little pressure but has fairly small occupants. A 10-inch rainbow would be extremely large. This is a good stream to keep in mind if heavy rain has blown out fishing in Little River, Middle Prong of Little River, and Abrams Creek.

Laurel Creek
(East Prong of Little River tributary)

This Laurel Creek is the one that most visitors know as Laurel Falls. The one-mile trail from the parking area is paved all the way to Laurel Falls. This is perhaps the most visited trail in the Smokies. However, the stream is among the least fished. Access is generally poor.

The best way to access the creek is to walk on the Quiet Walkway between the Elkmont intersection and the Laurel Falls Trailhead. Once you get in the creek, the only way to go upstream is to stay in the stream.

Rainbows are what you should expect but you may be surprised a good brookie, bu these brookies are not the native Southern Appalachian fish. They were stocked above the falls many years ago in an attempt to make a new population. Biologists were not aware of the genetic differences at the time. Now they only try to restore populations with local fish. These northern brookies are not as prolific as the native ones, but do seem to grow a bit larger.

Little River—Roadside

Little River is easily the most popular stream in Great Smoky Mountains National Park and one of the prettiest trout streams in this part of the country. The river's winding nature produces many large pools and long runs. A fisherman will have to look far and wide to find a wild Appalachian trout stream that has as much to offer. In fact, the stream was counted among Trout Unlimited's top 100 trout streams in America. There is plenty of water to be fished from the convenience of a car. There is also ample opportunity for back-country fishing. Few streams produce

Little River is home to many fine rainbows and browns that will take dry flies or nymphs. Spring and fall are the best times to hook the best fish.

as many large brown trout. It could be argued, though, that other park streams could produce equal numbers of good fish if they were fished as much. Little River is the regular haunt of many of East Tennessee's best fly fishermen and its trout are among the park's best educated.

Since this stream is fished more regularly than other park streams, fly consideration is a little more critical here than other mountain streams. Traditional attractor patterns like Royal Wulffs are effective, but tend to lose their potency as the season wears on. More realistic patterns will be more reliable by the time Memorial Day rolls around. Never forget, though, that an unrealistic fly presented perfectly will be far more effective than a realistic pattern presented poorly.

In the lower reaches near Townsend, Little River holds good numbers of smallmouth and redeye bass in addition to rainbow and brown trout. At the forked intersection known as the "Y", the East, Middle, and West Prongs of Little River combine before leaving the national park. This stretch of river is composed mostly of deep pools that can be difficult to wade and fish. Winter and spring flows are generally high. Swimmers and tubers will crowd this area in the summer. More productive water will be found upstream. There are occasions, however, when this piece of water can be productive. At least a few April and May evenings will yield excellent hatches or spinner falls. Oftentimes light cahill mayflies will be joined by little yellow stoneflies. The fish may only be eating one or the other, so be sure to pay attention.

Making a left turn at the "Y," the East Prong of Little River heads upstream toward its headwaters below Clingman's Dome and Mount Collins. The East Prong is generically known as Little River. The road follows the old railroad bed that once transported timber from the area. Locals have given many of the pools and runs names, but the name you get for a pool depends on who you ask. Places like Metcalf Bottoms and the Sinks are recognized on maps. Some rapids like Bottoms Up, Mary's Rock, and the Elbow were named by whitewater paddlers and are

known to a few fishermen by these names. Other places, like the Baptizing Pool and Indian Head, were named long ago by residents, and yes, people are occasionally baptized in the Baptizing Pool. A ranger could direct you to the Sinks but would probably scratch his head if you asked where the April Pool was.

The lower part of the river, extending from the park line to the first bridge that crosses the East Prong, can be extremely tough fishing. This is the roughest section in the Little River Gorge. Banks are steep, pools are deep, and the rapids are swift. Dry flies aren't as effective as they are further upstream. Streamers can produce well at times. This is one part of the river where a spin fisherman can often out perform a fly fisherman. This area is particularly tough in the summer when water temperatures occasionally exceed 70 degrees. These summertime temperatures favor members of the bass family, not the cold water dependent rainbow and brown trout. While difficult, this part of the river can be rewarding. Smallmouth bass may be caught from the same pools and runs as trout. Late winter into spring is the best time of year to fish this section. Nymph fishing is the dependable way to go, but dry flies can be effective on spring days and evenings.

From the point where Meigs Creek tumbles over its namesake falls into Little River, trout fishing can be a bit more reliable. The combination of classic dry fly pools and rough pocket water seems to favor trout over bass. (Bass are present as far upstream as the Sinks, but in small numbers.) Rainbow and brown trout are the only game fish upstream of the Sinks. This is also the point that anglers should consider the starting point for reliable trout fishing in the summer months.

The Sinks is one of the most recognizable pools on the river and known to almost anyone that has spent much time on Little River. This deep pool is bounded by high rock ledges and lies at the bottom of the largest waterfall on the river. Whitewater paddlers consider it a rite of passage to run the rapids into the pool, thrill seekers jump off of the rocks into the pool, and fishermen try to imagine what swims in its emerald depths. One Wears Valley fisherman caught a twenty-nine inch brown trout at the Sinks some years ago and by all accounts that fish was not the first or last big one to reside there.

If you pay careful attention, you will notice that the rocks at the waterfall are jagged, not smooth like other rocks in the river. During the logging era, this spot was blasted to redirect the flow of the river. The rocks at the waterfall haven't been weathered for thousands of years like the rest of the river.

There are relatively few turnouts between the Sinks and Metcalf Bottoms Picnic Area which can make this a somewhat private stretch of water if you make the effort to walk from your vehicle. The long pools at Metcalf Bottoms are popular but difficult. The water is smooth and slick and even the most careful wader can spook fish. In the summer this is a popular place for picnicking, swimming, and rock skipping. Fishermen should show up here early or late in the day when the crowds are thin and the trout more active. Also, the pools just above and just below the picnic area are worth scouting. This whole stretch of water is some of the best dry fly water to be found anywhere during the spring and fall.

About a mile-and-a-half upstream of Metcalf Bottoms the river plunges into a gorge as it flows under Long Arm Bridge. The base of the ridge that the river traces is named Long Arm. Wading should be done with caution in this section as it contains some of the fiercest white water on the river. Some of the finest trout habitat on Little River can be found from approximately Long Arm bridge to Elkmont Campground. The combination of gentle stream gradient and ideal water temperatures makes this area of the river the most prolific. There are even good populations of bait fish to satisfy the appetite of brown trout with a carnivorous appetite.

Elkmont was once a thriving logging town complete with a train station and post office. The deserted Wonderland Hotel and some empty summer cabins on Little River and Jake's Creek are the only remnants of that era. It is hard to look at this area and identify many of the places seen in old photographs taken in the 1920s. It is even harder to look at the forest surrounding Elkmont today and reconcile it with the photos of mountainsides stripped bare by log skidders.

Little River—Back Country

Upstream of Elkmont, Little River takes on a new character. Access is only by the Little River Trail and pools become rarer. Most of the water is rough, with tumbling pocket water that harbors mostly rainbow trout. Browns are present, but their numbers are dramatically less than they are downstream.

Just like anywhere else in the park, any trout over nine inches is a good fish and one over 12 inches is extraordinary.

Trout of this size can be found but make up a small portion of the population. While large brown trout are rare in this part of the river, they do exist. Take heart in the fact that if your fly does drift over a nice fish, chances are good that it will be eaten. These trout do not see the number of fishermen that their downstream brethren do and are a bit more naive.

Upstream of Fish Camp Prong the stream is not very big, but allows more than enough casting room for the experienced Appalachian fly fisher. The stream is composed almost entirely of rainbows but there are still enough browns to keep things interesting, especially if it's one of the rare 16 inchers that are occasionally reported. Most of the fish here are willing to consider a dry fly and will definitely accept a variety of nymphs and wet flies.

A back-country campsite at the confluence of Rough Creek and Little River is an ideal place to pitch a tent and explore the upper reaches of the river because this part of the river is tough to fish in a day trip unless you're in good shape and get an early start. The best way to explore this area is to backpack in and spend a few days. From this spot, one can explore upper Little River, Fish Camp Prong, or Rough Creek.

The bulk of the water upstream of Elkmont is pocket water. Nice trout could be in unlikely looking lies.

The complexion of the stream remains the same until it splits into its headwater prongs at the point known as Three Forks. The chances of catching a brook trout get better, though remain unlikely.

Everything upstream of Three Forks is closed to fishing. The trail ends here at back-country Campsite #30. The terrain becomes much steeper at this point, so steep that loggers couldn't negotiate it to cut timber. The trout between Rough Creek and Three Forks are as willing as I've found. That's the best reward for packing in.

Lynn Camp Prong

At the end of Tremont road, the Middle Prong of Little River splits into its two headwater tributaries, Lynn Camp and Thunderhead Prongs. After crossing the foot bridge at the parking area, Lynn Camp is on the left. These are predominantly rainbow trout waters. However, the very rare brown may be caught downstream of the impressive Lynn Camp Cascades. (The cascades are nearly 80 feet high.)

Lynn Camp Prong is popular with horseback enthusiasts, although few are fishermen.

Lynn Camp is a fine stream and its occupants are rarely picky, especially if you invest 30 minutes of walking before fishing. Brook trout are present in tributaries and are a possible catch after a good hike upstream.

The best opportunities for brookies are above the split with Indian Flats Creek where Lynn Camp is relatively hard to approach. Lynn Camp Prong forks about

Lynn Camp Cascades

two-and-a-half miles above the Middle Prong Trailhead. Lynn Camp Prong is to the left and Indian Flats to the right, yet this fork is easy to miss. Lynn Camp steers away from the trail for some distance before rejoining the trail. Lynn Camp Prong is closed upstream of back-country Campsite #27.

Mark's Creek

Mark's Creek is a tributary to Lynn Camp Prong which flows in across the stream from the Middle Prong Trail so spotting it may be difficult. This highly overgrown stream is difficult to locate and harbors a mixed population of rainbows and brookies. Rainbows are the most prevalent in the lowest reaches of this stream. While some may consider this type of fishing fun, it is too claustrophobic for others.

Middle Prong of Little River

The Middle Prong of Little River is often referred to as Tremont, which is what it was called during the logging era. Before that, it was known as Walker's Valley for William Walker who settled it in the 1850s. The Little River Logging Company bought it from him when he was on his death bed in late 1918. This was among the last areas of the park to be logged with the last logs hauled out in 1938.

The Middle Prong begins high on the slopes of Thunderhead Mountain to the west, and Cold Spring Knob to the east. The two major headwater tributaries that merge to form the Middle Prong are Thunderhead Prong and Lynn Camp Prong.

The Middle Prong is easily divided into two sections, the lower two miles bounded by asphalt road and the next two miles followed by gravel road. The lower section is composed mostly of long runs and pools with pocket water in between. This part of the stream is best in March and April during the height of the spring hatches. As the year progresses into the heat of summer, this part of Middle Prong is best passed by for upstream destinations. This lower part of the stream is inhabited by a few smallmouth and redeye bass which seem to be most evident May through September.

The gravel road section of Tremont is easily the most popular with fishermen. The water in this part of the creek is an even distribution of pools, pockets, and runs. When conditions are prime, Middle Prong is like trout soup. Bushy dry flies are favorites with trout and trout fishermen at Tremont, but don't neglect nymphs. There are days when it seems a bead head nymph couldn't get through a nice run with an armed guard.

Most of the fish caught will measure seven inches or less with a few going nine to twelve inches. Rainbows are

Tremont's beautiful pocket water and greedy trout make it a favorite with Smoky Mountain fishermen.

the predominant species but there are enough browns to keep you guessing. There is also the possibility of catching a stocked trout that has run upstream from Townsend. These rainbows will be larger than the stream bred trout, and will usually be far less colorful and have damaged fins. Browns at Tremont will be larger on average than the more plentiful rainbows. Some of the largest browns ever caught in the park have come from this innocent looking stream, with at least one weighing in at over 10 pounds.

Mill Creek

Mill Creek merges with Abrams Creek at the Abrams Falls Trailhead. Upstream, it flows past its namesake grist mill at the Cades Cove Visitor Center.

The rainbows in Mill Creek are not typically as tough to fool as those in Abrams Creek. However, if you're looking for larger fish or more casting room go to Abrams Creek.

Panther Creek
(Lynn Camp Prong tributary)

This very small stream enters Lynn Camp Prong near the Panther Creek Trail. The rainbows will generally be small but aggressive. Considering that fishermen are usually few and far between this far up Lynn Camp Prong, this stream should only be considered an enjoyable diversion for small stream fanatics in the area but not necessarily a destination.

Panther Creek
(Abrams Creek tributary)

Panther Creek enters Abrams Creek just before it enters Chilhowee Lake proper. In fact, the lower section of

Panther Creek is a narrow cove on Chilhowee Lake. Fishing at this elevation is marginal at best. Spring fishing in the lake embayment is good for redeyes and smallmouth but creek fishing for trout can be tough.

An unofficial path follows the creek upstream from the lake but keep in mind that it is not maintained and any storm that brings down trees can make future travel tough.

Fishing on Panther Creek improves as you move farther upstream but is hardly worth the tremendous effort. Spring is the best time to make a trip to Panther Creek because the slim possibility of run-up trout from Chilhowee Lake is at its best. There is a barrier falls about a half mile above the lake and any trout from Chilhowee will be below this point. However, the best reason to visit this stream is for the pleasant boat ride.

Further upstream Panther Creek flows under Parson Branch Road which exits Cades Cove. It is an extremely small and tight stream at this point. There is no defined path so fishing any distance up or down from the road can be a troublesome undertaking.

Parson Branch

Parson Branch flows along Parson Branch Road, a one-way road that exits Cades Cove and terminates at Highway 129. In order to reach the small Parson Branch, you must pass Little River, Middle Prong of Little River, West Prong of Little River, Laurel Creek, Anthony Creek, Abrams Creek, Mill Creek, and Forge Creek. Any of these streams are equal to, or better than, Parson Branch. Anyone that is a small stream fanatic will enjoy this stream, though. You may consider parking where Parson Branch flows under Highway 129 and walk upstream to fish. From this point the creek flows a little over a mile to its end at Calderwood Lake. This section is outside of the park and requires a Tennessee fishing license that includes trout.

Rabbit Creek

Rabbit Creek is a tributary of Abrams Creek that is among the least fished streams in the park. The reason for this is good, however. Its confluence with Abrams Creek is over three miles from the trailhead at Abrams Creek Campground. After that kind of hike the fishing in Abrams Creek is often more rewarding than what is found in Rabbit Creek. This part of Rabbit Creek is best fished if you plan to spend several days at Campsite #17 on Abrams Creek. It is not very far away and can be a pleasant diversion. Keep in mind though that Rabbit Creek is a marginal fishery thanks to its relatively low elevation. It fishes best after several years of wet, mild weather. Drought years are especially hard on this stream.

The best way to access Rabbit Creek is from the Rabbit Creek Trail that starts at Abrams Creek Campground. It is about a three-mile walk that finds the stream at Campsite #15. There is no path up or down the creek so you will have to use the stream bed to navigate, but you can be reasonably assured that you will have it to yourself.

This stream does flow under Parson Branch Road but may easily be mistaken for a drain ditch so don't bother.

Rough Creek

Rough Creek is a good but small stream that merges into Little River near Campsite #24. If you have to choose after a long hike, Rough Creek shouldn't be your first pick of the choice between it and Little River. Small rainbows will make up the bulk of your catch, but there are a few browns in the lower stretches of the creek. The best way to explore this stream is to establish a base camp and compare your fishing at Rough Creek to that of Little River, and possibly nearby Fish Camp Prong.

Spruce Flats Prong

Spruce Flats spills over three large waterfalls before it enters the Middle Prong of Little River about one mile up the gravel part of Tremont Road. Although beautiful, there are no trout upstream of the falls.

Tabcat Creek

Tabcat is one of those streams where I hope this book saves you some trouble. Access is only afforded by a small boat or a grueling off-trail walk through briars and deadfalls. Fishing for redeyes or the occasional good smallmouth in the Tabcat embayment of Chilhowee Lake is the only reason to bring a rod. Trout may be present in the headwaters, but considering the size of the stream and the tremendous effort that would be required, I could think of countless options that would be far more productive.

Thunderhead Prong

Thunderhead Prong joins Lynn Camp Prong to form the Middle Prong of Little River at the end of Tremont Road. Thunderhead gets less pressure than Lynn Camp since there is less trail access.

Rainbows are the predominant species. I once caught a small wayward brown, but have heard of very few others ever caught there. An occasional brookie down from Sam's Creek may also be caught here.

Although it is a small stream Thunderhead provides plenty of nice plunge pools and enough space to cast.

After about a mile, the trail turns from Thunderhead and follows Sam's Creek. At this writing Sam's Creek is closed to fishing. However, it is the subject of brook trout restoration efforts and may eventually be opened.

Fishing Thunderhead upstream of Sam's Creek will require coming back the way you came. There is an old rail bed above the stream, but it has become so overgrown as to be impassable in several places.

West Prong of Little River

West Prong is one of the most easily accessed streams in the park but one of the most overlooked by seasoned trout fishermen. This stream is easily accessed by car along Laurel Creek Road which goes to Cades Cove.

Rainbows make up the entire game fish population, with the odd brown or redeye bass in the lower pools. West Prong leaves the road about two-and-three-quarter miles above the Townsend "Y." Above this point, there is no official trail access. However, there is a very well-beaten path that a few dedicated fishermen use.

The West Prong Trail intersects the stream at Campsite #17. This is the only campsite on the stream but it receives light use in spite of its relative ease to reach. Rainbows in the back-country section of West Prong are small but aggressive.

More Helpful Books for Fishing and Fly Tying

THE BENCHSIDE INTRODUCTION TO FLY TYING
by Ted Leeson & Jim Schollmeyer

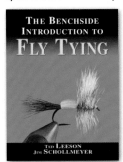

Ted Leeson and Jim Schollmeyer have set another milestone in the world of fly tying with this unique new addition to their Benchside Reference series. Following the incredible success of *The Fly Tier's Benchside Reference*, Jim & Ted now offer the first beginner's book of fly tying to allow readers simultaneous access to fly recipes, tying steps, and techniques. The first 50 pages of this oversized, spiral-bound book are filled with impeccably photographed fly-tying techniques. The next 150 pages are cut horizontally across the page. The top pages show tying steps for dozens of fly patterns, including references to tying techniques that are explained step by step in the bottom pages. Over 1500 beautiful color photographs, 9 X 12 inches, 190 all-color pages.

SPIRAL HB: $45.00   ISBN-13: 978-1-57188-369-8
UPC: 0-81127-00203-0

THE FLY TIER'S BENCHSIDE REFERENCE TO TECHNIQUES AND DRESSING STYLES
by Ted Leeson and Jim Schollmeyer

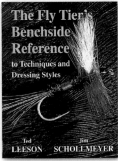

Printed in full color on top-quality paper, this book features over 3,000 color photographs and over 400,000 words describing and showing, step-by-step, hundreds of fly-tying techniques! Leeson and Schollmeyer have collaborated to produce this masterful volume which will be the standard fly-tying reference book for the entire trout-fishing world. Through enormous effort on their part they bring to all who love flies and fly fishing a wonderful compendium of fly-tying knowledge. Every fly tier should have this book in their library! All color, 8 1/2 by 11 inches, 464 pages, over 3,000 color photographs, index, hardbound with dust jacket.

HB: $100.00   ISBN-13: 978-1-57188-126-7
UPC: 0-81127-00107-1
CD: $59.95 For PC or Mac   ISBN-13: 978-1-57188-259-2
UPC: 0-66066-00448-2

CURTIS CREEK MANIFESTO
by Sheridan Anderson

Finest beginner fly-fishing guide due to its simple, straightforward approach. It is laced with outstanding humor provided in its hundreds of illustrations. All the practical information you need to know is presented in an extremely delightful way such as rod, reel, fly line and fly selection, casting, reading water, insect knowledge to determine which fly pattern to use, striking and playing fish, leaders and knot tying, fly tying, rod repairs, and many helpful tips. A great, easy-to-understand book. 8 1/2 x 11 inches, 48 pages.

SB: $9.95   ISBN-13: 978-0-936608-06-8
UPC: 0-81127-00113-2

FLY-FISHING NEW JERSEY TROUT STREAMS
by Matt Grobert

This book is the culmination of 35 years of experience, information, insights, observations, and the wonders of fly-fishing for trout in the Garden State. Written with the passion of a life-long fly-fisherman, you will gain valuable knowledge on becoming a better angler and naturalist no matter where you fish for trout. Coupled with the lyrical narrative are dozens of photographs taken by a variety of New Jersey anglers who share the author's love of fly-fishing for trout. Matt covers every aspect of fly-fishing for trout in New Jersey with a style and clarity to suit every level of ability. You will learn about three species of trout and their behavior, the rivers they live in, the tackle to catch them, the insects they eat, and the artificial flies that imitate those insects. 6 x 9 inches, 88 pages, full-color.

SB: $19.95   ISBN-13: 978-1-57188-417-6
UPC: 0-81127-00251-1

TENNESSEE TROUT WATERS: BLUE-RIBBON FLY-FISHING GUIDE
by Ian Rutter

There is tremendous diversity in Tennessee's trout waters: tailwater rivers, mountain streams, and lakes, and much of it is on public land. This guidebook will give you a good starting point for exploring these waters, including up-to-date information, detailed maps, and easy-to-understand icons. Productive techniques and fly patterns are given for over 25 different trout waters, as well as what species you can expect, whether hiking is required, available camping and accommodations, whether it is safe for canoe, drift boat or motorized boats, and more. Not only is Tennessee beautiful and historical, it has great trout fishing: Tennessee Trout Waters is your guide. 8 1/2 x 11 inches, 86 pages.

SB: $22.00   ISBN-13: 978-1-57188-294-3
UPC: 0-81127-00121-7

FLY-FISHING TECHNIQUES FOR SMALLMOUTH BASS
by Harry Murray

If you want exciting fishing with hard-fighting fish, go for smallmouth bass. If you want to learn from the master, go to Harry Murray. Drawing on a lifetime of fishing, guiding and teaching at his angling schools, Harry covers all aspects of fly-fishing for smallmouth bass in a way that benefits anglers of all skill levels. You will learn about: tackle; casting; smallmouth water; minnow-matching tactics; nymph fishing; taking smallmouth on the surface; floating a smallmouth river; fishing for smallmouths in lakes and ponds; and more. 6 x 9 inches, 120 pages, all-color.

SB: $19.95   ISBN-13: 978-1-57188-360-5
UPC: 0-81127-00194-1
HB: $29.95   ISBN-13: 978-1-57188-362-9
UPC: 0-81127-00196-5

TYING & FISHING SOFT-HACKLED NYMPHS
by Allen McGee

Trout often prefer underwater aquatic insects because they're more vulnerable than surface stages and are more abundant as well. Fly-fishers know the importance of imitating the specific life stage that trout are feeding on, however most current flies only imitate size, shape, and color of the natural insect. Soft-hackled nymphs also imitate movement and behavior. *Tying & Fishing Soft-Hackled Nymphs* explains how to imitate sub-surface aquatic insects using both traditional and modern soft-hackled nymphs and flymphs along with the most effective presentation techniques. By exploring effective thread and translucent fur body material combinations, as well as game-bird hackle collars, these flies take on life-like properties. These patterns can be fished throughout the water column from the stream bottom—to imitate immature nymphal forms—to the surface mimicking transitional emergers. Drawing on both traditional and evolved patterns and methods, these wingless wet flies will take you beyond formulaic fishing techniques to unlimited presentation possibilities and will help you catch more trout. 8 1/2 x 11 inches, 96 pages.

SB: $24.95   ISBN-13: 978-1-57188-403-9
UPC: 0-81127-00237-5

TROUT STREAM FLY-FISHING
by Harry Murray

The purpose of this handy little guide is to enable you to refine your angling skills so you can enjoy fishing for trout on streams anywhere in the country. Murray has decades of experience fishing small streams, and shares important information such as: trout foods and fly selection; reading water; spotting trout; techniques for all seasons; mastering all water conditions; trout behavior and habitat; fly tackle; fly casting; hatches; fly plates; and more. 4 x 5 inches, 102 pages.

SB: $9.95   ISBN-13: 978-1-57188-281-3
UPC: 0-81127-00100-2

OZARKS BLUE-RIBBON TROUT STREAMS
by Danny Hicks

Ozark streams are exceptionally rich in nutrients that create big trout, Danny Hicks provides detailed information on this region's great fishing. This book covers all the Ozarks' year-round trout fisheries, and concentrates on the tailwaters and largest spring-fed rivers. Hicks includes: fish species, primary trout foods, all the different waters you'll encounter in the region, productive techniques for the Ozarks, fly choice, best approaches, equipment, weather, access, and more. 8 1/2 x 11 inches, 88 pages.

SB: $19.95   ISBN-13: 978-1-57188-163-2
UPC: 0-66066-00361-4

Ask for these books at your local fly/tackle shop or call toll-free to order:
1-800-541-9498 (8-5 p.s.t.) • www.amatobooks.com
Frank Amato Publications, Inc. • P.O. Box 82112 • Portland, Oregon 97282

0061